A Field Guide to Hot Sauces

A FIELD GUIDE TO HOT SAUCES

A Chilehead's Tour of More than 100 Blazing Brews

Todd Kaderabek

drawings by Christi Teasley

EDITOR: **Deborah Morgenthal**
ART DIRECTOR/PRODUCTION: **Chris Bryant**
ILLUSTRATIONS: **Christi Teasley**

Library of Congress Cataloging-in-Publication Data

Kaderabek, Todd.
A field guide to hot sauces : a chilihead's tour of more than 100 blazing brews / Todd Kaderabek : illustrated by Christi Teasley.
p. cm.
Includes index.
ISBN 1-887374-10-8
1. Cookery (Hot pepper sauces). 2. Hot pepper sauces. I. Title.
TX819.H66K33 1996
641.8'14—dc20 96-20181
CIP

10 9 8 7

Published in 1996 by Lark Books
50 College Street
Asheville, NC 28801

Distributed by Random House,Inc.,
in the United States, Canada, the United Kingdom, Europe, and Asia

Distributed in Australia by Capricorn Link (Australia) Pty Ltd.,
P.O. Box 6651, Baulkham Hills Business Centre, NSW 2153, Australia

Distributed in New Zealand by Tandem Press Ltd.,
2 Rugby Rd., Birkenhead, Auckland, New Zealand

Printed in Hong Kong

ISBN 1-887374-10-8

Contents

Introduction

ALL RIGHT, *who died and made me hot-sauce king? No one, and I hope you will never be blessed or cursed with this title either. However, somewhere along the line, I began to amass a collection of hot sauces that was the source of some embarrassment and occasional financial, as well as gastronomical, discomfort.*

It all may have begun when I was four or five, lying in a hospital bed in Loyalton, California, suffering the effects of too much Tabasco at too young an age. Or maybe it was the spicy fish tacos on the Baja coast I indulged in when I was a kid. Or it could have been the presence of Leo Leyva, spouse of my piano instructor, who constantly distracted me from my études by spoon-feeding himself from a bowl of wickedly hot green salsa. Whatever the onset, I have had a lifelong love affair with hot sauce, and while this doesn't make me king, it may at the very least allow me the privilege of playing court jester.

This love used to be a simple matter, uncomplicated by habañero relish and jalapeño lollipops. Not the case today. Go into just about any grocery store and you'll see

at least a dozen and probably more choices in the condiment section. Actually, most stores today have so many choices that hot sauce has earned its own section, and rightfully so. However, with choices come confusion, duplication, and a generally muddled mess that can lead to "I think I'll try that" turning into "Why in God's name did I try that!" Thus, a common source of information seems important so that you the buyer can avoid spending your hard-earned money on tomato sauce labeled as salsa or vice versa.

So was born The Field Guide to Hot Sauces. *This book is not intended as all encompassing, all informing, or all anything. It is intended for the sole usage of those of you who want adventurous advice from someone who has tasted most of it, and lived to tell about it. Take this book with you. Put it in your glove box. Pack it in your suitcase. Make notes in it, good, bad, or otherwise, and pass this information on to friend and foe alike, depending upon your desired effect. Most of all, have fun with it. Life is too short to be uptight about hot sauce.*

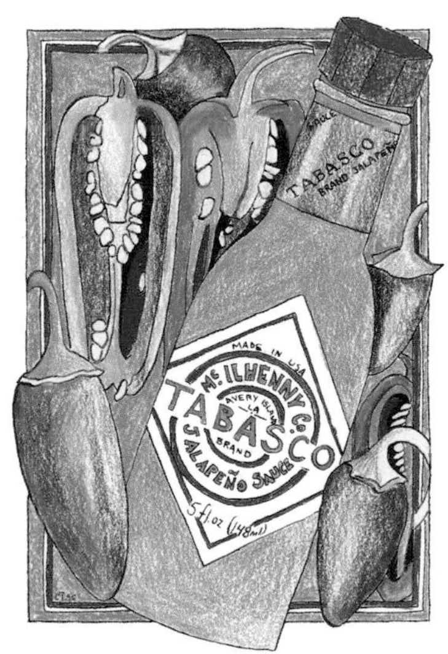

Glossary of Peppers

There sure are plenty of peppers mentioned in this book! Here is some inkling of what is what, and tastes like which, and is otherwise somehow relevant. Please keep in mind—I'm not the Pepper God, nor do I play Him/Her on television. These are merely my observations based on my experiences with the peppers and sauces mentioned in this book, plus a bit of research done while waiting on a lot of laundry.

Ancho (Poblano)

One of the most common peppers to be found in sauces from Mexico, it is grown widely across Mexico, and can also be found in the pepper fields of Southern California. Termed poblano when green, and ancho when it becomes greenish black, this pepper will eventually mature to a bright shade of red. The skin is tough in the poblano stage and must be removed prior to usage. It is mild in heat, although this varies a good bit from pepper to pepper.

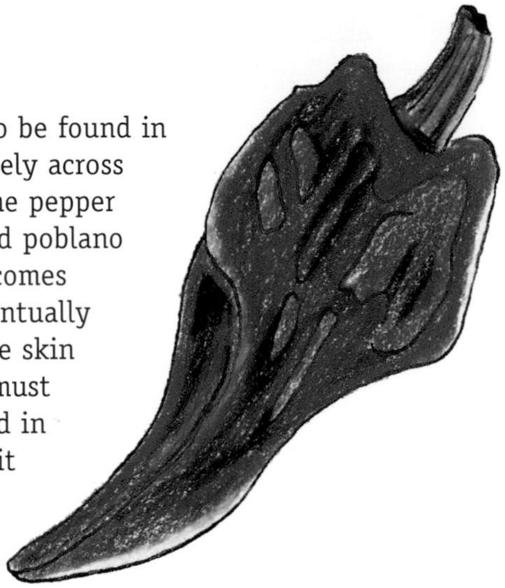

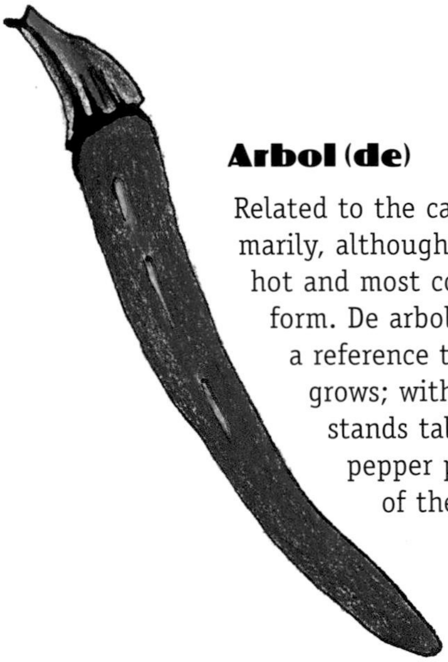

Arbol (de)

Related to the cayenne, this pepper is grown primarily, although not widely, in Mexico. It is fairly hot and most commonly ground into a powdered form. De arbol is literally "treelike" in Spanish, a reference to the manner in which the plant grows; with a woodlike stem, the arbol plant stands tall—more like a tree than some pepper plants that stagger under the weight of their fruit.

Banana

The banana pepper comes in two distinctly different levels of heat, both disguised coyly as the mild form, or actual banana pepper. The impostors are Hungarian hot wax peppers, which may explain why your occasional salad garnish is mild one time, hot the next. Most grocers don't differentiate between the two, and these peppers definitely can vary within one bin. Mostly seen in its yellow (banana) form, this pepper does eventually mature to a beautiful stage of red. Extremely easy to grow, it tastes good pickled.

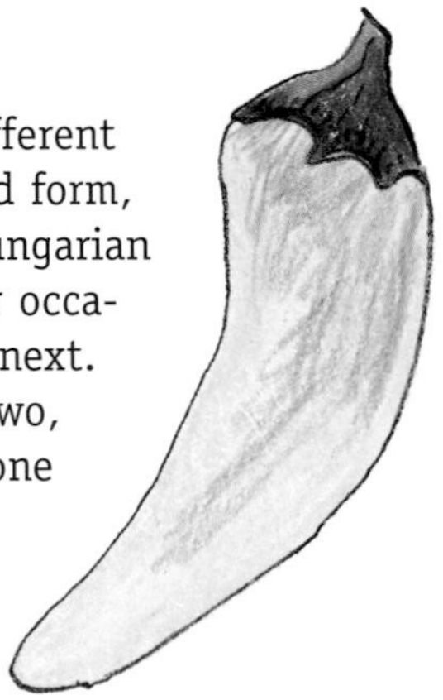

Glossary of Peppers

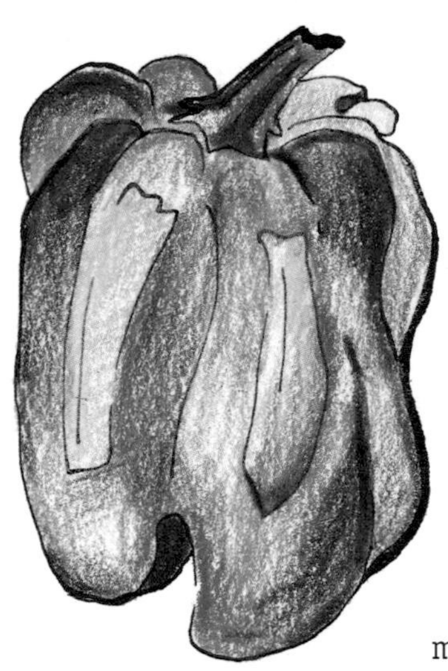

Bell

Obviously, the name is derived from the shape of the pepper, which is clearly that of a bell. This is a very mild pepper, and comes in a variety of types, all of which are large and fleshy. It is used in sauces primarily as filler or to stretch out a recipe for little cost, although bell peppers do add flavor, notably with little to no heat infused. Definitely for the meek at stomach.

Black Pepper

Surely you jest?

Bonney

Botanically speaking, this is not a type of pepper. The term Bonney seems to be a way to wipe that evil grin off the face of the habañero or other dangerously hot peppers and is used infrequently to distract unwary hot heads from the matter at hand. What? Yeah, yeah... hell, I have no idea!

Glossary of Peppers

Cayenne

The most common form of chile pepper found in America, this is mostly used in ground, dry form, although it is found in a variety of pepper sauces. It is also referred to as green chile or red chile pepper. Named for the Cayenne River in French Guiana, where it is supposed to have originated, it is grown now primarily in North America and Europe and, notably, not in South America at all. A hot pepper, with long burn potential, the plant is easy to grow, and small enough to be potted and grown inside, where it will produce peppers all winter.

Cora

Similar to the de arbol and not widely grown.

Datil

Grown exclusively in the St. Augustine, Florida, area, this pepper is fairly rare, and only recently have datil seeds become available to home growers. First grown in Florida by the Minorcan exiles, this pepper is said to be related to the habañero. It packs a lot of the heat in its small greenish yellow pod. Use sparingly if you can get your hands (gloves) on a few of them.

Guajillo

Nearly translucent when dried, clusters of this pepper are sometimes strung as ristras or pepper garlands; in this form, it is often termed cascabell as well. Referred to as mirasol in its fresh form, the guajillo is a medium-heat pepper grown primarily in Mexico, but it will do well in your garden if you have a long growing season.

Glossary of Peppers

Habañero

Literally "from Havana," this hottest of the hot is said to have been first cultivated in Cuba, although some evidence points toward South America, specifically Colombia. Although generally unspeakably spicy, its heat index can vary drastically depending on the amount and intensity of sunlight received during the growing season. This can be troublesome in northern climates, but it is still possible to have good success cultivating habañero plants with an early enough start and some ultraviolet lamps. Though it is difficult to describe, but worth noting nonetheless, the habañero has a highly distinctive flavor that can be appreciated both before and after you light your gills on fire.

Hawaiian Chile

Any of the little known (especially to me) variety of chiles grown in the more well known area of Hawaii.

Jalapeño

The best known of all chile peppers, the jalapeño is grown in Mexico and in the more arid climates of the United States. It is of a medium to hot nature and is characterized by a sharp flavor and an intensely long burn. Smoke dried jalapeños are known as chipotles.

Glossary of Peppers

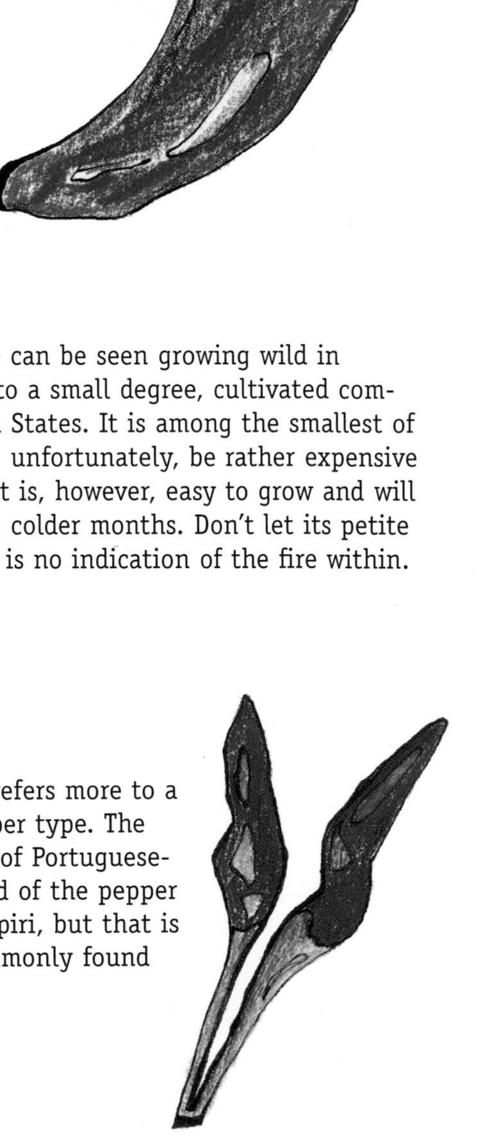

New Mexican

The giant of the chile world, this huge green pod matures into fire-truck red as the season progresses. Sometimes mislabeled as an anaheim, a true New Mexican is considerably hotter than its West Coast cousin, although it tends to vary from somewhat mild to leaning-toward hot. This is the deep red chile you most commonly see strung in ristras, although it is also widely used for culinary purposes and for good reason: lots of flavor.

Pasilla Negro

Same as ancho.

Piquin

This fiery hot little chile can be seen growing wild in coastal Mexico, and is, to a small degree, cultivated commercially in the United States. It is among the smallest of chile peppers and can, unfortunately, be rather expensive to purchase. The plant is, however, easy to grow and will do well inside during colder months. Don't let its petite stature fool you—it is no indication of the fire within.

Piri Piri

Literally "Pepper-Pepper," this term refers more to a style of sauce than to a specific pepper type. The sauce is described on page 68 and is of Portuguese-African descent; the same can be said of the pepper that is sometimes referred to as piri piri, but that is most closely related to the more commonly found Brazilian pepper type, malagueta.

Glossary of Peppers

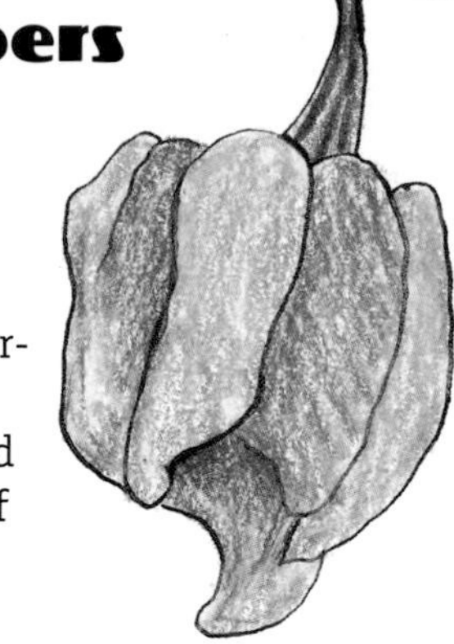

Scotch Bonnet

Identical to the habañero, but the term Scotch bonnet (Scot's bonnet, clearly a reference to the tam-shaped pepper's resemblance to the Scottish-style hat) is used in the English-speaking countries of the Caribbean.

Serrano

This is the best of the gardeners' chiles—prolific and easy to grow in a multitude of climates. It is medium hot and most commonly used to make salsa, but you will occasionally see these peppers pickled. The serrano has a unique flavor that has added to its popularity in America, a fact which increases its availability.

Tabasco

This pepper is not native to Avery Island, Louisiana, as is widely supposed, but rather to Tabasco, Mexico, where it has grown for centuries. This small chile is very hot and should be handled with care. A nice addition to many dishes in its fresh form, the tabasco is perhaps best used to make hot sauces and salsas; it doesn't fare well when dried. Plants are reasonably easy to grow and are very attractive in the garden, resembling small apple trees brimming with ripe, red fruit.

Tepin

Also chiltepin, a variation of the piquin.

Thai

Clearly native to Thailand, a Thai pepper plant produces some of the smallest and hottest peppers around. Yes, these are those little things floating around in your Thai cuisine that force you to excuse yourself from the table and take the next day off from work. This pepper isn't grown much commercially in America, but it's a good bet to grow on your own and makes a great addition to stir-fry dishes. It also combines nicely with tabasco peppers to make an interestingly flavored river of fire.

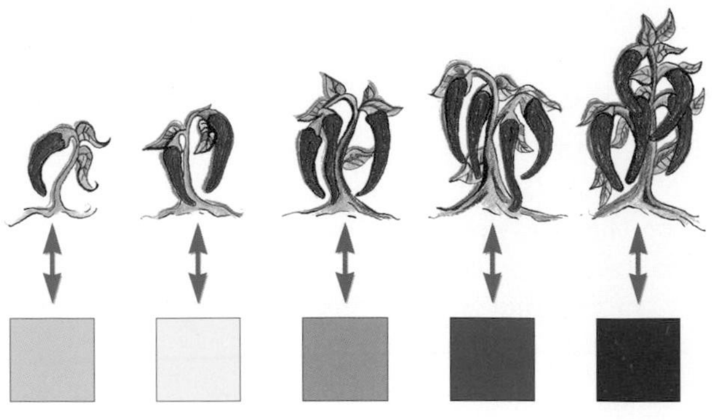

HOTNESS INDEX

The hot sauces is this book are arranged into five sections, each one representing my subjective measurement of how hot each sauce is. Within each section, the sauces are listed in alphabetical order—the idea being that you should be able to easily and quickly find a particular hot sauce, unlike what happens when facing the mayhem in my refrigerator.

The heat index of each section is indicated in two ways; you'll see a small pepper plant on the bottom of each page with either one, two, three, four, or five peppers growing on it: all the plants with one pepper are grouped in the same section.

In case this is too subtle, you'll also find a small color bar on each page under the pepper plant and behind the page number at the top of the page; a different color is used in each section to indicate how much you can expect your tongue to be singed by the sauces in that particular section. The first section (one pepper) is lime green, the second (two peppers) is yellow, the third (three peppers) is orange, the fourth (four peppers) is orange-red, and the fifth (five peppers) is bright red. Get it? Okay, then get on with it. And don't say we didn't warn you in every way we know how.

Bufalo Jalapeño Mexican Hot Sauce

A product of Mexico, distributed by Festin Foods Corporation, Carlsbad, California, 92009

Ingredients: Water, carrots, vinegar, red jalapeño peppers, sugar, salt, cellulose gum, sodium benzoate, artificial color

Comments: Don't expect to get stampeded by this Bufalo: the label says extra hot, but it's not. A slightly too sweet red sauce that is a bit too close to ketchup for my taste. Decent spice flavor, but otherwise blah.

Bandana's Seriously Cilantro Pepper Sauce

Bandana's Inc., P.O. Box 110, St. Peter's, Pennsylvania, 19470
■ 215-286-7986

Ingredients: Vinegars, onion, carrot, garlic, habañero peppers, cilantro

Comments: If you like cilantro, add this one to your collection — you do have a hot-sauce collection by now, don't you? Otherwise, this is a fairly forgettable sauce. Very thin, not very hot, this is one of those sauces that really should be great, but for whatever reason, just misses the mark. For the mild-mannered fan of cilantro and few others.

Cajun Chef Brand Louisiana Hot Sauce

Cajun Chef Products, Inc., St. Martinsville, Louisiana, 70582

Ingredients: Selected Louisiana cayenne peppers, distilled vinegar, salt, cellulose gum, food color

Comments: Down the bayou from Louisiana Gem, Cajun Chef does good work. What a difference a few blocks and a few good peppers make. This is one of the quintessential Louisiana sauces—not very hot, but still spicy and with a ton of character. As with most Louisiana hot sauces, it's readily available and mighty cheap. Load up your next plate of oysters with this one.

Cajun Chef Brand Louisiana Green Hot Sauce

Cajun Chef Products, Inc., St. Martinsville, Louisiana, 70582

Ingredients: Selected Louisiana cayenne peppers, distilled vinegar, salt, xantham gum

Comments: If you're on a low-sodium diet, I suggest you stay away from this one. But if you're a salt junky like me, check this one out. This is one of my favorite green sauces and it's loaded with salt—the saltiest sauce I've tasted, balanced perfectly with a hearty dose of peppers. I love it and think you will too. (Did I mention that it's salty?)

Cajun Power Garlic Sauce

Cajun Power Sauce Manufacturing, Inc., Rt. 2, Box 278, Abbeville, Louisiana, 70510 ■ 318-893-3856

Ingredients: Vinegar, tomato purée, a blend of imported and domestic spices, garlic, seasoning, sucrose, natural flavoring, salt, cayenne peppers, xantham gum

Comments: If you love garlic, and I do, then this sauce is for you. Not spicy, but bursting with fresh garlic taste, this sauce makes a great addition to Italian tomato sauces or to just about anything else you might find on the plate in front of you—or the plate next to you, for that matter.

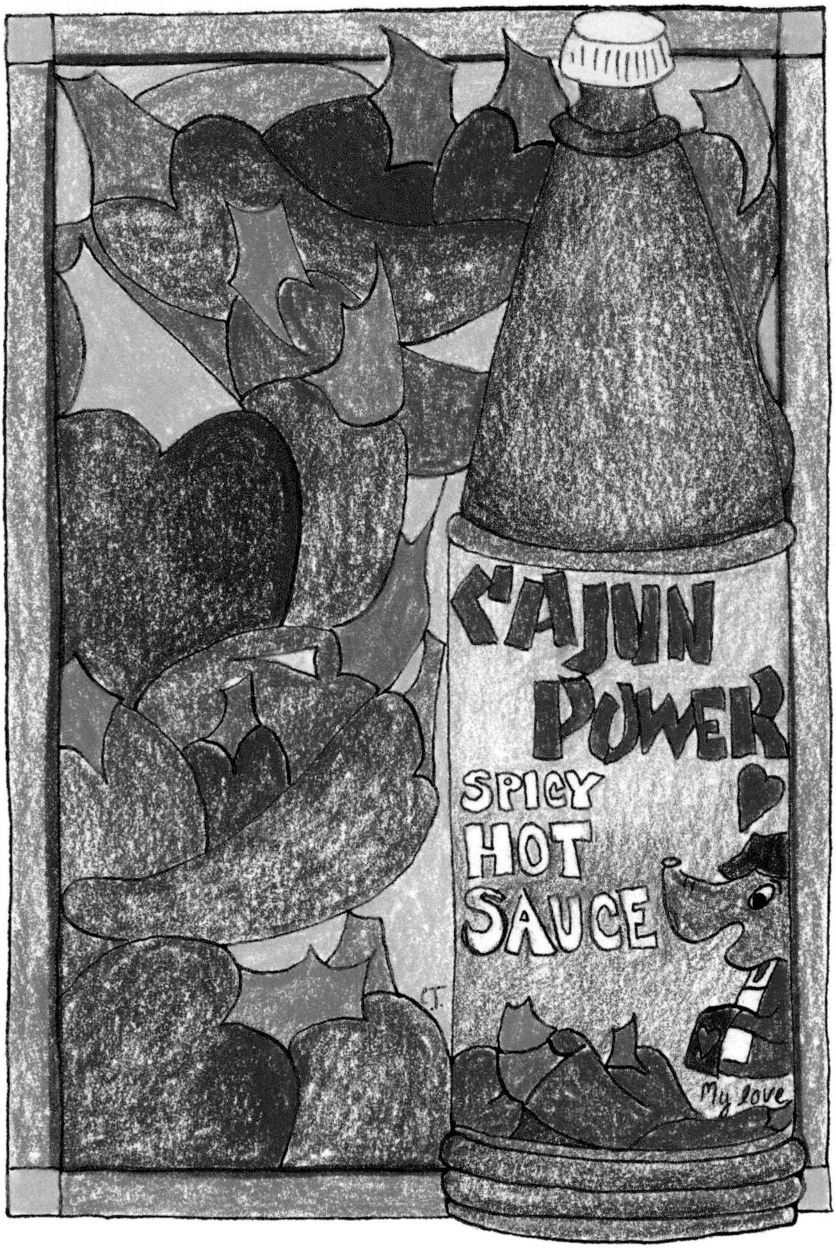

Cajun Power Spicy Hot Sauce

Cajun Power Sauce Manufacturing, Inc., Rt. 2, Box 278, Abbeville, Louisiana, 70510 ■ 318-893-3856

Ingredients: Red ripe peppers, vinegar, tomato purée, spices, garlic, seasonings, sucrose, salt, natural flavoring, food stabilizer

Comments: Another great product from our friends at Cajun Power, who guarantee this sauce to be 100 percent Cajun, whatever that means. The "freshly squeezed" garlic in this sauce is at the forefront of the fantastic flavor of this not too spicy but very tasty offering. Very comfortable in the center of every table, and more than comfortable on the palate.

Coyote Cocina Tangy Taco Sauce

Coyote Cocina, 1364 Circle #1, Santa Fe, New Mexico, 87501 ■ 800-866-HOWL

Ingredients: Red chile, vinegar, fresh garlic, tomato paste, modified food starch, salt, approved spices, natural flavors, red coloring #40, sodium benzoate

Comments: As your basic taco sauce, this is a good choice. Not very hot, but that isn't always the idea, is it? The big New Mexico reds in this are bursting with flavor. Mark Miller serves up another sauce to be reckoned with.

Dat'l Do-It Datil Pepper Hot Sauce

Dat'l Do-It, P.O. Box 4019, St. Augustine, Florida, 32085 ■ 800-HOT-DATL

Ingredients: Tomato paste, water, fructose, datil peppers, vinegar, lemon juice, honey, salt, spices, garlic

Comments: This is a good all-around sauce, a little sweet, not very hot—your grandmother could eat this one and live to tell about it. Datil peppers are grown in and around St. Augustine, the oldest city in America, and have a deep, rich flavor that in this sauce is pleasing but not powerful. Try their Devil Drops for a spicier variation.

(kăp′sĭ kəm) = hot!

Capsicum, Schmapsicum!

All right, let's get right to and then right off the point. Capsicum refers to a genus of plants, most of which used to be tropical but are now grown all over the world. The term is also used to describe the active ingredient of pepper plants, which is what we are after here. It is also followed in my dictionary (*American Heritage, Second College Ed.*) by capsid: the proteinaceous covering of a virus particle. These definitions are all about as relevant to me. Heat, it means heat to me!

First of all, capsicum is a sort of difficult word to remember, let alone to remember to say correctly. So, when you hear people using it without stumbling, or at least pausing to see if they are going to be corrected, they are either master gardeners, who have every right to use the term, or people who talk the talk but probably don't walk the walk.

The next time you hear someone blathering on about capsicum, ask them if they think capsids would be more resistant to modern medical technology if treated with capsicum? And then ask them to pass the hot sauce.

Becoming More Tolerant

If you persist, you will become tolerant, so says the Eighth Principle of Hot Heads, or some other such ballyhoo. It is true though, that over the years, your palate will learn to accept and appreciate hotter and hotter dishes. This isn't to say, however, that there will come a time when you will be unaffected by eating raw habañeros; if this happens to you, let me know, and I'll send the men with the rubber suit to pick you up.

After 25 years of self-inflicted torture, I still sweat beyond comprehension, hiccup to the point of seizure, and otherwise embarrass my wife and friends on rare public outings. Still, I enjoy it immensely, live to tell about it, and come back another day to eat hot sauce.

Which brings me to my long awaited point here: start out slow and mild and pick up steam as you feel comfortable. No sooner than you should bungee jump nude from the Statue of Liberty's nose should you be pressured into trying sauces clearly off your scale. If sympathy is your thing, go out and break your arm with a vise, as you'll get little to no sympathy from chileheads. Take it easy and you'll soon advance from just saying no to just saying thanks.

Salt on Your Tail

If you are adding hot sauce to your favorite recipes that call for salt, check the label. If salt is listed as an ingredient, consider it already added. If you're on a low-sodium diet, you should keep in mind that there are plenty of sauces without salt in them. Shop carefully and you can find many salt-free brands that are full of flavor.

Gib's Bottled Hell Hot Pepper Sauce

R.& B. Enterprises, 175 Weaverville Highway, Asheville, North Carolina, 28804, or P.O. Box 5278, Louisville, KY 40255 ■ 800-881-5233

Ingredients: Tomato paste from red, ripe tomatoes, distilled vinegar, chili peppers, jalapeño peppers, banana peppers, onions, green bell peppers, corn syrup, salt, onion powder, spices, herbs, natural flavorings

Comments: It's not surprising that a sauce from North Carolina serves better as a barbecue sauce than a hot sauce, and trust me, they are "cuein" it up out on Weaverville Highway. That's okay though, as this makes for a great spicy rib sauce, even if you never dip a chip in it. The 12-ounce bottle makes it economical, so slather it on and grill, baby, grill!

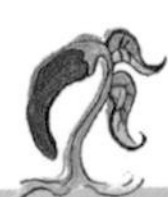

Hammonds Jamaica Style Hot Pepper Sauce

Hammonds of Yorkshire, Apperly Bridge, Yorkshire, BD10 Oly, England; distributed in the U.S. by Reese Finer Foods

Ingredients: Tomatoes, mangoes, sugar, malt vinegar, fermented soy protein, molasses, salt, tamarind purée, acetic acid, chili pepper, lactic acid, dehydrated onions, spices, caramel, dehydrated garlic, artificial flavor

Comments: This is a very complex sauce, as you might gather from the extensive list of ingredients. It will be loved by some and not so well received by others. If you have a taste for fruitier sauces, this may be the ticket, and it is certainly one of the best English sauces on the market. Try it on your next batch of Yorkshire pudding, or better yet, douse it all over your bangers and mash (ouch!). It makes a pretty decent steak sauce, too. Also an excellent addition to Bloody Marys, as well as to your morning eggs.

Hooters Hot Sauce

Hooters Foods Incorporated, 2471 McMullen Booth Road, Suite 316, Clearwater, Florida, 34619

Ingredients: Red peppers, vinegar, salt, brown sugar

Comments: This may be the only politically correct way for males to sample Hooters sauce without encountering the wrath of female friends. Long known for their spicy chicken wings, Hooters disappoints here with a chicken of a sauce. A novelty product to be sure, this five-ounce bottle won't last long if you're looking for heat. If you can stand eating amongst nearly naked women (I cannot), try the wings at Hooters, but leave the sauce on the grocery shelf.

Horse-Shoe Louisiana Red Hot Sauce

Horse-Shoe Pure Foods, a division of Rex Pure Foods, Inc.,
New Orleans, Louisiana, 70130

Ingredients: Cayenne peppers, distilled vinegar, salt, food stabilizer

Comments: New Orleans is chock-full of fun and decadent things to pursue; this is not one of them. It's a very standard Louisiana red sauce found all over the state, probably prepared from one recipe, and perhaps cooked all in one pot! This isn't to say that it's bad—it's okay, but very common. If it's less than a buck, and you're very low on options, buy it; otherwise, shop on for more interesting sauces.

Louisiana Gem Hot Sauce

Acadiana Pepper Company, Inc., St. Martinsville, Louisiana, 70582

Ingredients: Red peppers, distilled vinegar, salt, guar gum

Comments: The good news: this sauce comes in a huge bottle—17 ounces and is very inexpensive. The bad news: it is not worth it! This sauce lacks any distinctive quality and may be bottled in such large quantities just so they can get rid of it and go home. Unless it's free or close to it, and the only sauce on the planet or close to it, avoid this "gem." One possible use: dog bite repellent.

Louisiana's Pure Crystal Hot Sauce

Baumer Foods, Inc., P.O. Box 19166, New Orleans, Louisiana, 70179

Ingredients: Aged cayenne peppers, distilled vinegar, salt

Comments: I've got a real thing for truck stops—I love everything (well, almost everything) about them, but especially the food, followed closely by the restroom graffiti. And at most truck stops, you can find a bottle of Crystal; so, I like it as well. But, in all honesty, it's not that great. Or, maybe it is—give it a try. Just make sure you do so in a good, old-fashioned truck stop, preferably on a lengthy road trip, with your dog, in an old convertible, heading west...

Louisiana Southern Spice Hot Sauce

Southern Spice, Rt. 2, Box 148, Lake Providence, Louisiana, 71254
■ 318-559-1774

Ingredients: Water, aged pepper mash, distilled vinegar, salt, cellulose gum, artificial colors

Comments: As you may have noticed, there is no shortage of hot sauce coming out of Louisiana. Most of them share some common tendencies, most notably the usage of peppers, salt, vinegar, and not much else. Thus, they also share a common thread in flavor, heat, etc. So, if you've already got a Louisiana sauce or two or three, wait until one runs out to buy this one. Good but nothing special, this is one of those run-of-the-mill mild sauces it's nice to have around for less adventurous diners.

Outerbridge's Original Hot-Concentrated Bloody Mary Fix

Outerbridge Peppers, Ltd., P.O. Box FL85, Flatts 3, Bermuda

Ingredients: Sherry, peppers, lemon juice, spices

Comments: Not exactly a hot sauce, but hey, I make the rules here, so bear with me on this one—it's worth it. This is something you simply must have if you're going to fix Bloody Marys; its flavor is like no other I've tried, and the combination of sherry and hot peppers is sheer inspiration. Keep it a secret, and you'll be the toast of your friends. Makes a good steak sauce as well.

Panola
Cajun Jalapeño Sauce

Panola Pepper Corporation, Rt. 2, Box 148, Lake Providence, Louisiana, 71254

Ingredients: Cayenne peppers, jalapeño peppers, vinegar, salt, spices, guar gum

Comments: This is the green version of their red version—they should have stuck with the red. There's nothing special about this sauce; it's as likely to please as disappoint—take your chances.

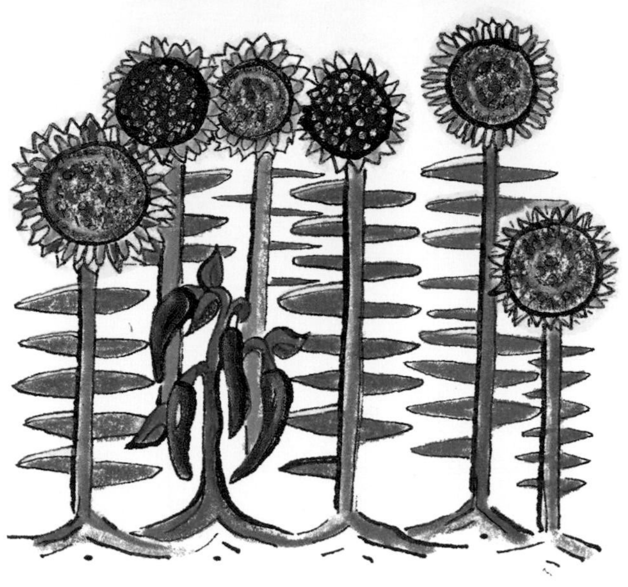

Grow Your Own

Peppers are something that, armed with a little good advice, even an inept gardener can successfully grow. And once you've grown your own, you will certainly snicker at the price of fresh peppers at the farmer's market.

RULE NUMBER ONE: Start early—February if you can remember—especially with habañero seeds, which are impossibly slow to germinate.

RULE NUMBER TWO: Because germination rates are low, plant far more seeds than you would ever want to grow into plants.

RULE NUMBER THREE: In early spring, when the seedlings are four to six inches high (or smaller—if you're like me and always seem to space out in February and wake up in mid-March) place them outside in small starter pots. Don't leave them out there indefinitely—an hour of sun the first day, two the next, four the following, and finally for a full eight hours. Then plant them in the ground on the fifth day. Choose the sunniest spot possible, afternoon sun being highly desirable as far as peppers are concerned.

THE FINAL RULE: Water them when they go in the ground and not again for a week, and continue to be stingy with the water. Unlike Californians, peppers love a good drought; a generous watering every ten days or so is usually sufficient, although if they are drooping to the ground, you might up the timing a bit.

With some care, such as ridding them of spider mites, (try Dr. Bronner's Magic Peppermint Soap, diluted heavily and misted onto the leaves) which are very fond of peppers, and careful usage of nonchemical fertilizers (remember, you're going to eat these), you should end up with a yard full of beautiful, tasty—and if you get plenty of summer sun—very hot peppers that will be the envy of your neighbors, or at least further proof that you are indeed nuts, as seems to be the opinion on my street.

Pee Wee's Cajun Cayenne Juice

La Cour de Ferme, Ltd., 1019 Delcambre Road, Breaux Bridge, Louisiana, 70517 ■ 318-332-3613

Ingredients: Cayenne peppers, vinegar, salt, jalapeño peppers, honey, cane syrup, brown sugar, garlic, onions, Worcestershire Sauce, lemon juice from concentrate, maltodextrin, natural butter flavor acid, butter, buttermilk solids, corn starch, partially hydrogenated soybean oil, natural and modified gums, F.D.& C. yellow #5, spices

Comments: This sauce is as eclectic as the back roads of Louisiana where it was born, and just as worthy of your time. The everything-but-the-kitchen-sink recipe melds into a bottle full of flavor, not quite like any other, but bearing some of the parts of all the others. If you can't make any sense of this, you're doing better than I am—just go out and get a bottle, and apply with reckless abandon.

Pepper Creek Farms Wildfire

Pepper Creek Farms, Inc., Lawton, Oklahoma, 73501

Ingredients: Red peppers, apple cider vinegar, horseradish, garlic, sugar, salt

Comments: This is a unique sauce, an odd combination of ingredients that adds up to plenty of flavor, but not much heat. The addition of horseradish is a stroke of genius, as it provides the kick that this sauce needs. All natural, with no preservatives, keep this one well refrigerated, as those cider vinegar sauces seem to spoil easily.

Peppervine Fancy Hot Pepper Sauce

Peppervine, a division of Gourmet Foods, Inc., Knoxville, Tennessee, 37901

Ingredients: Vinegar, choice crushed cayenne peppers, pepper seeds

Comments: I try to avoid this type of sauce, a generic product of a large food company, often overpriced, and easily recognizable by the addition of pepper flakes, which incidently serve little more purpose than to clog up the bottle top. That's the story on this one—I should have known! However, it does have a decent piece of art work on the label, so there's the hook. If you're looking for art, put it on your kitchen shelf; otherwise, leave it on the store shelf.

Pickapeppa Sauce

The Pickapeppa Company, Ltd., Shooters Hill, Jamaica, West Indies

Ingredients: Tomatoes, onions, sugar, cane vinegar, mangoes, raisins, tamarinds, salt, peppers, spices

Comments: As you might have gathered from the ingredients, this is not a spicy Jamaican sauce at all, but rather a sort of mucked up fruit and vegetable sauce, with just a hint of pepper thrown in for goodness sake. And good it is, particularly stirred into Bloody Marys, or spread over grilled fish. There's plenty of heat in Jamaica—just not in this sauce, which is flavorful nonetheless.

Smokey Chipotle Hot Sauce

From the Kitchens of Montezuma

Sauces and Salsas, Ltd., 7856 Forest Brook Ct., Powell, Ohio, 43065

Ingredients: Chile chipotle, chile pasilla negro, water, distilled vinegar, fresh garlic, spices, salt

Comments: Said to have been derived from a Mexican recipe, this sauce, I'm afraid, has lost something in the translation. Although a deep brown-red color promises depth, it lacks any of the rich flavors of chipotles, those wonderful smoked red chile peppers. Rather, it comes up thin and wispy and has a frustrating tendency to separate. Still, if this is the only chipotle sauce in your area, and you've never tried one, you might give it a taste.

Spicy Capsicana Zing Gourmet Sauce

Home Industries, Inc., 3800 NC 86 South, Hillsborough, North Carolina, 27278

Ingredients: Vinegar, sugar, raisins, hot peppers, garlic, salt, spices

Comments: This was a gift from my mother-in-law, so I have to say it's very, very good. But, if it wasn't a gift from her, and seeing as she probably won't read this far into this silly book anyway, I have to say, it's NOT very, very good. The sauce is trying to be a Jamaican-style sauce (look at the ingredients), but it fails miserably. It's mostly sweet and mostly dull. So, if your mother-in-law gives you some, put on a happy face, and save it for later—much later!

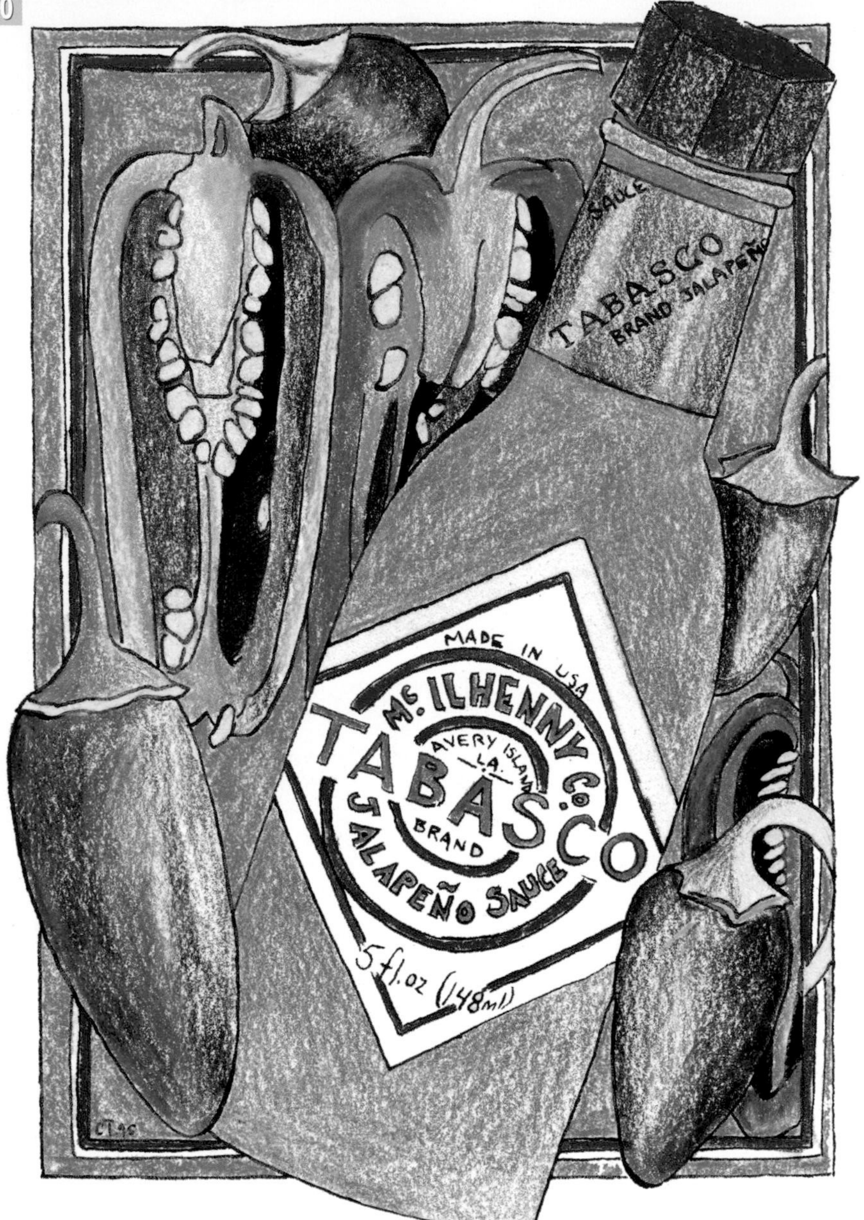

Tabasco Green Jalapeño Sauce

McIlhenny Company, Avery Island, Louisiana 70513

Ingredients: Vinegar, jalapeño peppers, salt, xantham gum, ascorbic acid, yellow #5, blue #1

Comments: Probably the closest I've come to having a heart attack was the day I spotted green Tabasco on the store shelf. I'm a purist of sorts, and messing with the messiah of hot sauce seemed like, well, it just seemed stupid. How wrong I was! This is the top of the heap of green sauces, with a distinctively fresh flavor and just the right amount of salt. Like the red stuff, it's easy to cook with, cheap, and a breeze to find. By the way, this product evidently is the result of the McIlhennys purchasing Trappey's—the times they are a changin'... My only complaint—yellow and blue might make green, but so do green jalapenos, and we probably could have done without the food coloring.

Tapatio Salsa Picante

Empacadora Tapatio, J.L. Saavedra, 2500 Fruitland Avenue, Vernon, California, 90058 ■ 213-587-8933

Ingredients: Water, red pepper, salt, herbs, spices, acetic acid, sugar, edible food stabilizer, sodium benzoate

Comments: This is a fairly decent sauce with hints of fresh herb flavors, reminiscent of some other Mexican-style sauces. Plenty of body, but a bit runny and mild. Not at the top of my gift list, but hey, who's giving it away anyhow?!?

Texas Pete Hot Sauce

T.W. Garner Food Company, Winston-Salem, North Carolina, 27105

Ingredients: Peppers, vinegar, salt, xantham gum

Comments: Call me crazy, but you just can't go wrong with a bottle of Texas Pete. Old Pete has saved me from many a vicious hangover and countless dull meals. It's one of my sentimental favorites, even if it is rather mild. I advise getting a quart or two, along with about ten pounds of chicken wings, and making a day of it.

Trappey's Bull Louisiana Hot Sauce

Trappey's Fine Foods, Inc., New Iberia, Louisiana, 70562

Ingredients: Hot red peppers, distilled vinegar, salt, edible food stabilizer, certified food coloring

Comments: I often find myself reaching reflexively for Trappey's Bull Sauce. There's nothing much special about it—I just have a soft spot in my stomach lining for it. It's a better sauce than a lot of its sister sauces, and just a tad hotter to boot. I like it. I guess we all need a little Bull now and then!

Trappey's Red Devil Louisiana Hot Sauce

Trappey's Fine Foods, P.O. Box 12638, New Iberia, Louisiana, 70562

Ingredients: Hot red peppers, distilled vinegar, salt, edible food stabilizer

Comments: A lot of these Louisiana red sauces are a-dime-a-dozen, or maybe we should be so lucky. But that doesn't mean they're without merit. Most of them are quite good, just similar to one another. That's the case here: nothing great, nothing bad, which can be good. If you're like me, people are always giving you hot sauce, for which I'm grateful. But every now and then, with all those red sauces piling up, you've got to throw in the towel, make a huge batch of spicy chicken wings, buy a bunch of beer, and invite all your friends over. Trappey's Red Devil is perfect for just such an occasion.

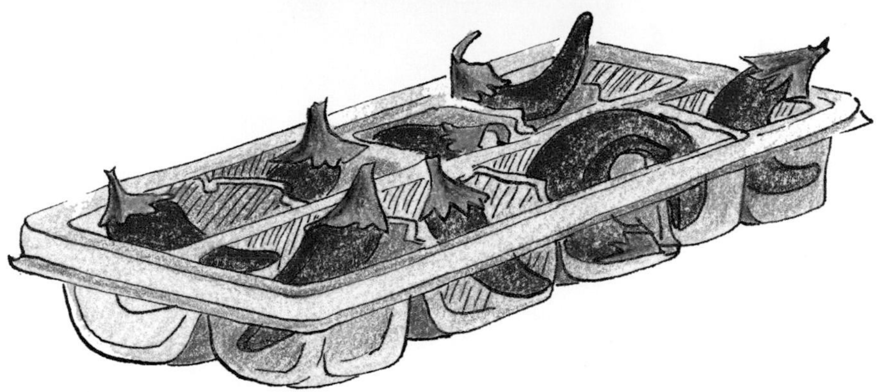

Frozen Chiles

So you went nuts and planted ten times too many pepper plants. Don't fret: you can freeze your chiles and use them later, much later. Sadly, many will be the people who didn't buy this book, who will wake their peppers one wintry day and find them dull, tasteless, and completely lacking in spice.

The secret: blanch them before you freeze them, and you'll have a spicy hot winter. See, aren't you glad you shelled out the cash for this silly book?

Salsas for Cooking

Not all salsas need to be fancy, filled with a myriad of obscure and interesting ingredients. I often set aside several pints of straight up, no-nonsense pepper brine (peppers blanched in vinegar, then pureed in the blender) to be used strictly for cooking and never for dipping.

Don't make the mistake of blanching your peppers in water; you must boil them in vinegar—even though your neighbors may complain that the aroma wafting on the breeze burned their nostrils. Peppers steamed in water and mixed with vinegar later separate in the jar, giving evidence to all of your skeptical friends that you really don't know what you're doing.

Spicy Chili?

Cool it off with cumin, a readily available and easily affordable spice. A couple of teaspoons in a gallon or so of your favorite recipe will put out some of the fire, and lend your concoction a taste of its own. You might also try thinning the heat with rice or, Cincinnati-style, with macaroni noodles. Still, once you're over the edge, it's hard to get back, and you may just have to live (or die, as the case may be!) with your lavalike bowl of chili.

Achiote Indian Sauce

Hot Heads, 639 East Marion Street, Lancaster, Pennsylvania, 17602

Ingredients: Liquid achiote, vinegar, water, chile tepin peppers, natural herbs, spices

Comments: This sauce has a unique and very pleasing flavor. Whatever an achiote is, it's not very hot, but it is the most brilliant red I've ever seen in a hot sauce made without government approved food dye. Actually, achiote is the seed of the Annotto tree, but what the hell is an Annotto tree? Who cares, just get some of this sauce, and you'll have all the information you need. Achiote? Bless you!!!

Across The Border Backfire (Tangy) Hot Sauce

Hill Country Food, Inc., Dallas, Texas

Ingredients: Purée of choice hot red peppers (tabasco, cayenne, and jalapeño), distilled vinegar, salt, edible food stabilizer

Comments: I try to give advertisers and label writers the benefit of the doutbt—but this sauce is NOT "tangy." How can it be tangy with no tangy ingredients?! Now that I've had my little tantrum, let me add that this stuff is pretty good—straight up, no frills heat (the trinity of peppers is a great idea). Enough said.

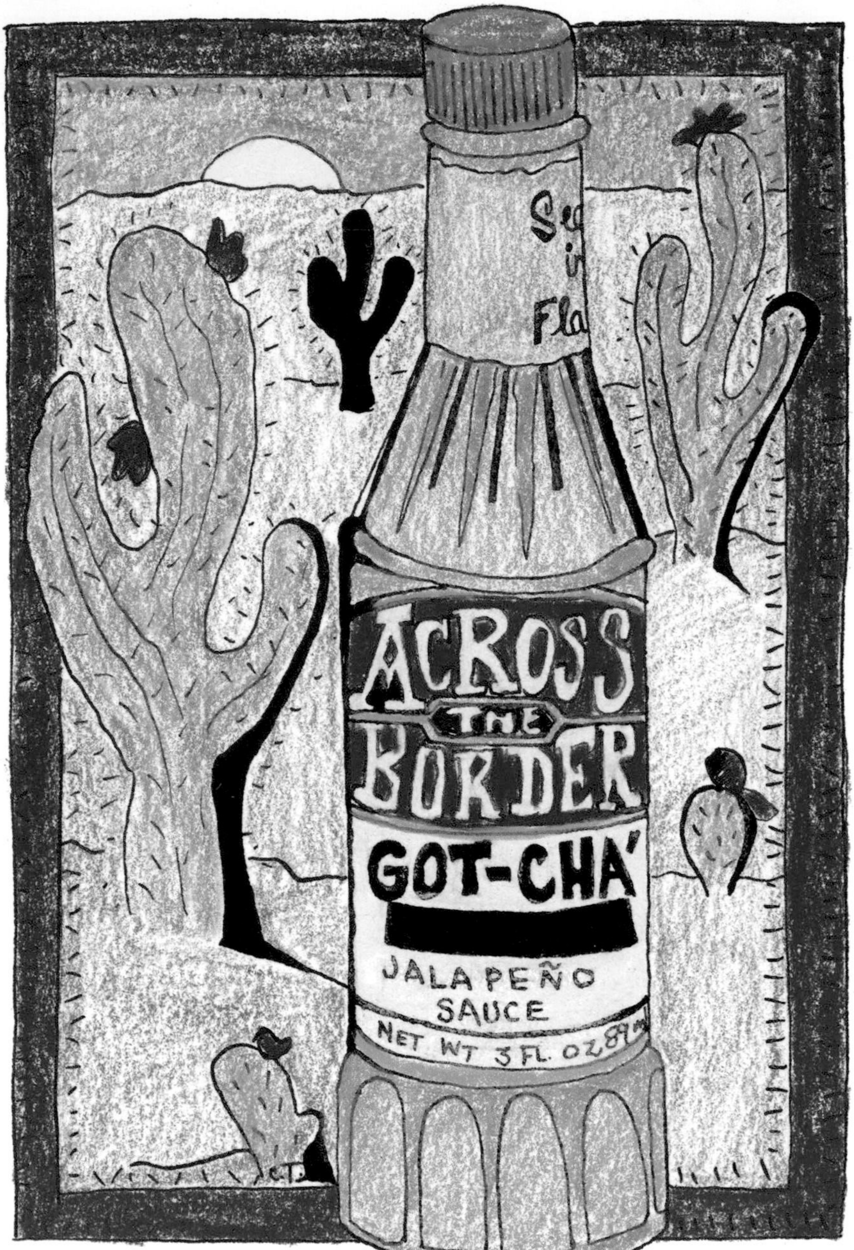

Across The Border Got-Cha' Jalapeño Sauce

Hill Country Food, Inc., Dallas, Texas, 75220

Ingredients: Purée of jalapeño peppers, distilled vinegar, salt, edible food stabilizer, F.D.& C. Yellow #5

Comments: This is an outstanding green Jalapeño sauce, with a good name to boot. Thicker than most greens, a pinch of this between your cheek and gum will go a long way. If jalapeños are your thing, this is the sauce for you.

Ana Belly Extra Salsa Picante

Alimentos Y Conservas, Ana Belly S.A., Guatemala, Central America

Ingredients: Select chile peppers, vinegar, salt, spices

Comments: These three-ounce bottles of fire come in a red and a green variety, and both are worth trying. The green version has a particularly fresh taste as if you've just sliced open a green chile straight from the field. The red is flavorful as well, although not as distinctive. Both sauces are a little thin, but this is a decent product from the pepper fields of Guatemala.

Arizona Gunslinger

Arizona Pepper Products, 638 West Broadway, Suite 302,
Mesa, Arizona, 85210 ■ 800-359-3912

Ingredients: Red ripened jalapeño peppers, vinegar, salt

Comments: Described as "Smokin' Hot Jalapeño Sauce," this six-ounce bottle packs some punch, without knocking your socks off. A thick and granular red sauce, this is a good choice for your friends who haven't graduated to habañeros yet but are past the steak sauce phase. Includes a good Buffalo Wings recipe on the back and plenty of flavor inside.

Ass Kickin' Hot Sauce

Southwest Specialty Foods Company, 5805 West McLellan #3, Glendale, Arizona, 85301 ■ 800-536-3131

Ingredients: Water, tomato paste, vinegar, crushed serrano peppers, salt, food starch, habañero pepper, fresh onion, fresh garlic, spices

Comments: Although serranos are the major flavor here—and a mighty good flavor at that—a pinch of habañeros gives this sauce its kick. Still, if you're really looking for "kick yo' ass hot," you'd better keep looking: this offering is a bit thin, a little grainy, and won't light your fire.

Cajun Rush Pepper Sauce

Cajun Rush, 22295 Gull Street, Maurepas, Louisiana, 70449
■ 504-695-6692

Ingredients: Hot peppers, vinegar, onion, garlic, herbs, spices

Comments: Leave it to those crazy Cajuns to come up with this sauce. One time I like it, the next time I don't—what am I gonna do?!? I think I'll keep it—and keep eating it. Try it, you'll like it, or maybe you won't, or maybe you will...

Casa Fiesta Hot Pepper Sauce

Bruce Foods Corporation, New Iberia, Louisiana, 70561

Ingredients: Fully aged peppers, vinegar, salt

Comments: Another Louisiana red sauce from the folks at Bruce Foods, this one disguised somewhat by its Spanish name, it is a very standard table sauce nonetheless. There's nothing wrong with it; as a matter of fact, it has a pretty good flavor (taking the time to age the peppers is a good sign) and a decent amount of heat. Still, nothing to mortgage the farm over.

Chef Han's Jalapeño Hot Sauce

Chef Han's Gourmet Foods, Inc., P.O. Box 3252, Monroe, Louisiana, 71210 ■ 318-322-2334

Ingredients: Jalapeño peppers, vinegar, salt, spices, cellulose gum, certified food coloring, F.D.& C. yellow #5

Comments: Not one of the best sauces out of Louisiana, but still darn good—and always cheap. According to the label, Chef Han was voted Restauranteur of the Year in 1986 by the Louisiana Restaurant Association. If you find out where he cooks now, let me know. In the meantime, this green sauce will do. Apply liberally and without fear.

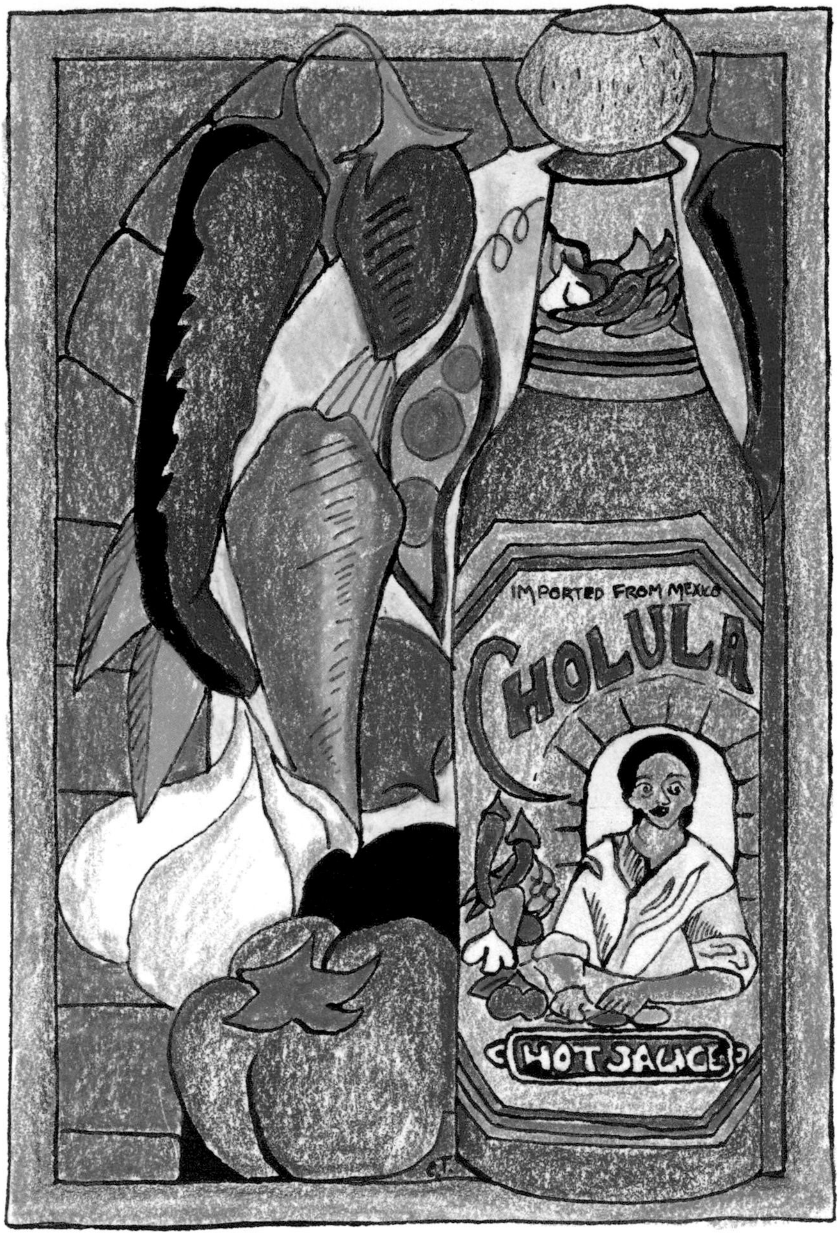

Cholula Hot Sauce

Sangrita De La Viuda De Sanchez, S.A., Chapala, Jalisco, 45900, Mexico

Ingredients: Vinegar, red peppers, piquin peppers, salt, spices, sodium benzoate

Comments: This two-ounce bottle with the distinctive wooden cap is easy to find in the United States and is a fairly decent hot sauce. The piquin peppers lend it a distinctive, sharp flavor, not found in most sauces on American shelves. Not great, but very respectable.

Community Kitchens Acadian Pepper Sauce

Community Coffee Company, P.O. Box 3778, Baton Rouge, Louisiana, 70821 ■ 800-535-9901

Ingredients: Jalapeño peppers, cayenne peppers, vinegar, water, onions, sugar, salt, spices, sodium benzoate

Comments: I don't know whether this is an actual old Acadian recipe or not, but it does have a hint of France about it. A little sweet, but very tasty, this is a great sauce to cook with or to use on its own. Some thought went into this Community Kitchens recipe, and it shows in the end product.

Community Kitchens Louisiana Green Hot Sauce

Community Coffee Company, P.O. Box 3778, Baton Rouge, Louisiana, 70821 ■ 1-800-535-9901

Ingredients: Jalapeño peppers, vinegar, onions, sugar, salt, spices, sodium benzoate

Comments: Community Kitchens has plenty of worthwhile and tasty products to offer, and this is a good example. The peppers in this sauce are very fresh, combined with not too much salt or sugar. A fragrantly nice flavor, and a pleasure to cook with.

Hawaiian Passion Fire Sauce

Hawaiian Passion, P.O. Box 1041F, Halewa, Hawaii, 96712

Ingredients: Water, cider vinegar, salt, Thai bird chiles, ginger, Hawaiian chile peppers

Comments: Hawaii is like no other state in America, and this is like no other American or foreign sauce. Perhaps the thinnest sauce I have ever tasted, it has a flavor so original it's worth a try for that reason alone. Thai chiles are rich in flavor, and the ginger and cider vinegar combine well. Shake it up, douse it on—weird.

Honky Tonk Devil

Cajun Chef Products, Inc., St. Martinsville, Louisiana, 70582

Ingredients: Selected Louisiana cayenne peppers, distilled vinegar, salt, cellulose gum, food color, other spices

Comments: The "other spices" are what set this sauce apart from the various other Cajun Chef products. A deep red color, this is one of the spicier and better Louisiana sauces around. The cackling devil on the label is a good indication of what lies within—as cayenne hot as cayenne gets!

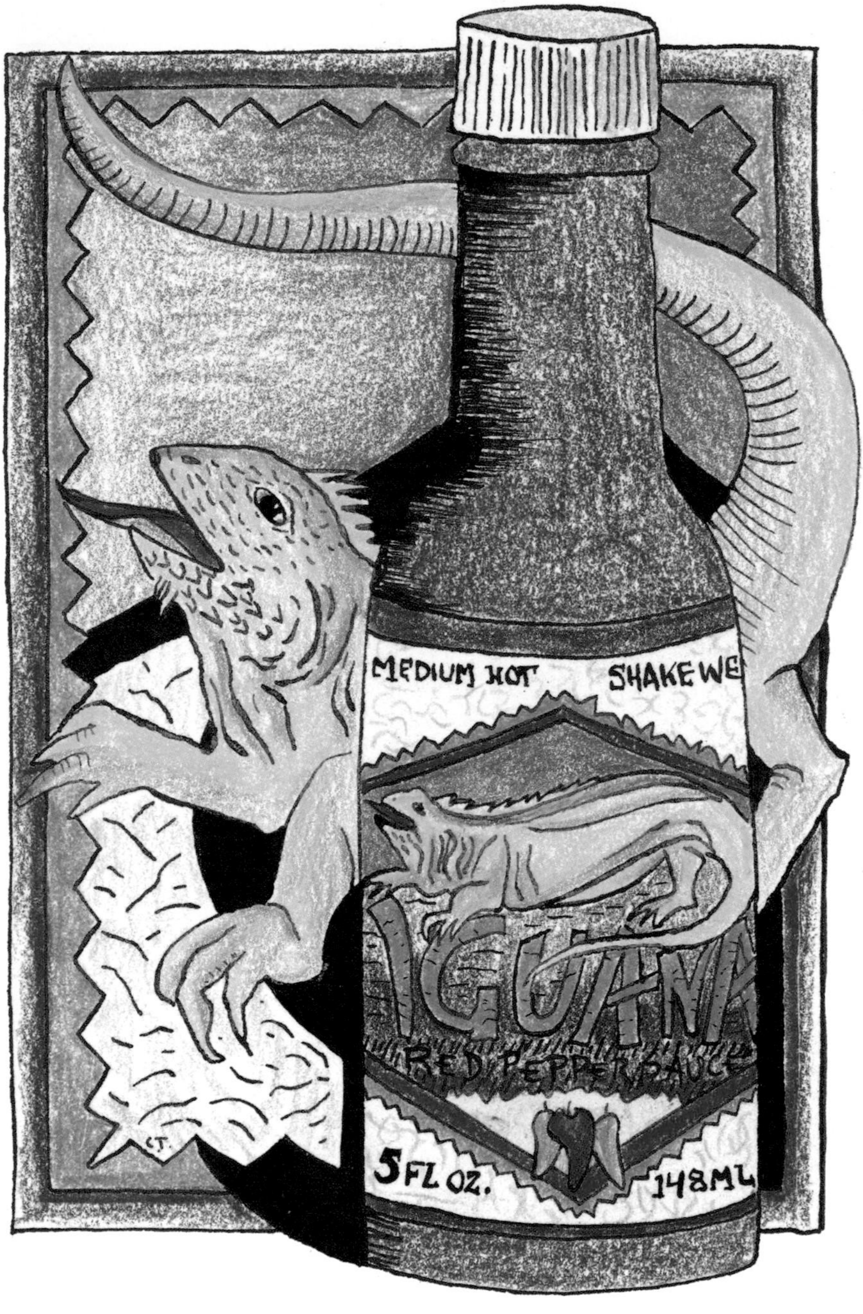

Iguana Red Pepper Sauce

A product of Costa Rica, imported by Half Moon Bay Trading Company, Jacksonville, Florida, 32202 ■ 904-356-7338

Ingredients: Cayenne peppers, carrots, tomato paste, onions, garlic, cane vinegar, cane sugar, salt, molasses, sodium benzoate

Comments: This sauce is said to be the result of "misadventure," but the end result is nothing of the sort—tangy, tart, and, as advertised, medium hot. I was wary of a sauce from Costa Rica that included tomato paste, but this product is good to the last drop.

Mini-Bottles and Pill Boxes

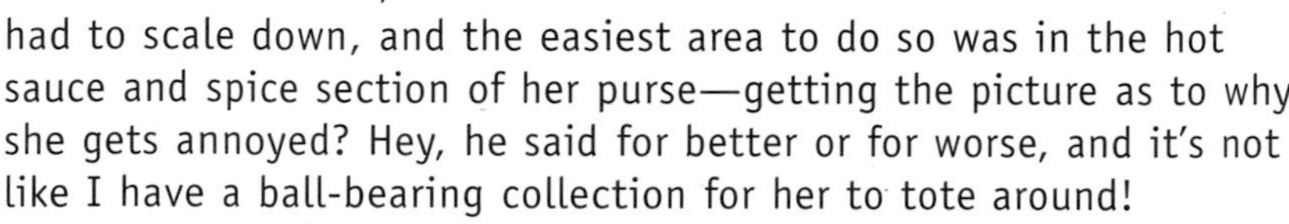

I'm constantly asking my wife to carry things for me in her purse, as I hate having pockets full of this, that, and the other.

Occasionally this leads to marital strife. So, I've had to scale down, and the easiest area to do so was in the hot sauce and spice section of her purse—getting the picture as to why she gets annoyed? Hey, he said for better or for worse, and it's not like I have a ball-bearing collection for her to tote around!

Anyway, mini-bottles of Tabasco Sauce are a great solution, and if you order enough hot sauce from most mail-order retailers, they'll throw in a few for free—yet another reason to order more hot sauce! These little guys often prove the difference between a meal to remember and a meal to gripe about on the way home. Also, they are easy to palm, and it isn't much of a trick to dash a little on without being noticed.

Along the same lines, pill boxes and vials can be filled with dried peppers and used in much the same manner—be careful not to breathe deeply immediately following overt application, or you'll be busy explaining your inexplicable sneezing spell.

Hot Socks

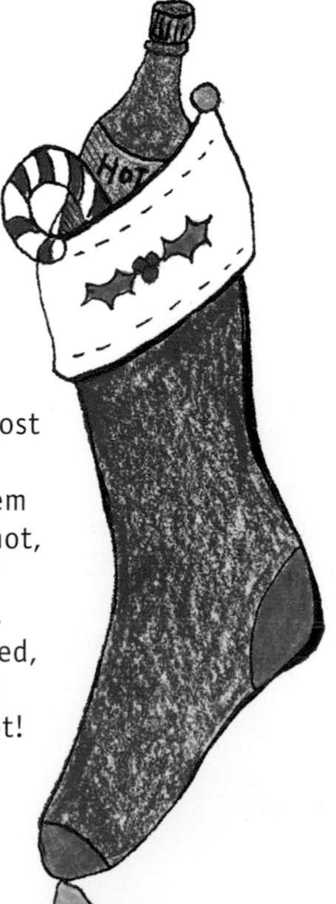

Hot sauces make great stocking stuffers (hint, hint) for that aunt, uncle, brother, or sister who just seems to have it all. Choose the most bizarre sauces you can find; if it's good, you can sponge some off them during the holiday season, and if not, they can chuck it in the privacy of their home after the merry making. This is also a decent, if underhanded, way to do some experimenting and still appear benevolent. Ho, ho, hot!

Inner Beauty—
Real Hot or Hot—Sauce

Made in Costa Rica for Inner Beauty, Inc.,
Cambridge, Massachusetts, 02139

Ingredients: Fruit juices, Scotch bonnet peppers, honey, onions, vegetable oil, mustard, curry, vinegar, corn starch, salt, flour, spices

Comments: This seven-ounce flask of Central American fire is a perennial (and perineal) favorite of chileheads, and for good reason. Its flavor is one of a kind, thick with mustard and curry, and plenty of Scotch bonnet heat as well. The back label warns, “This is not a toy. This is serious. Stand up straight, sit right, and stop mumbling.” Good advice. Made special for the folks at the East Coast Grill in Cambridge, in two degrees of heat to please most anybody.

Inner Beauty Hot Sauce

2 peppers

Inner Beauty Real Hot Sauce

4 peppers

La Guaca-Maya Hot Sauce

Industrias Guacamaya, S.A., DE C.V., Carr. A Navolato No. 9105 PTE., Col. Bachigualato, C.P. 80140, Culiacan, Sin., Mexico

Ingredients: Water, cora peppers, iodized salt, vinegar, spices, sodium carboxymethyl cellulose, benzoate

Comments: Cora peppers give this sauce a distinctive flavor, reminiscent of some ancho sauces, and the label makes a beautiful addition to any shelf. Not the hottest sauce you'll ever try, but one of the best, and a good gift for your bird-loving friends.

Lizano Extra Salsa

Manufactured by Productos Lizano S.A., Alajuela, Costa Rica; imported by Frank Macis, Macqui Produce, Inc., Los Angeles, California

Ingredients: Sucrose, mixed pickles, salt, spices, corn starch, hot peppers, acetic acid, hydrolyzed vegetable protein, sodium benzoate

Comments: It must have been a hot day indeed when the Lizano family thought up this crazy recipe. The only sauce I know of with mixed pickles, this product is surprisingly good (it leans toward sweet without going overboard), unique, and well worth going to some trouble to obtain. I would love to meet the Lizano family one day—they must be quite a daring bunch!

Lizano Seasoning and Cooking Sauce

Lizano S.A., Costa Rica

Ingredients: Water, vegetables, sugar, salt, vinegar, spices, cayenne peppers, hydrolyzed vegetable protein, sodium benzoate

Comments: Throw away the A-1 and stock up on this delicious Costa Rican sauce, a family recipe of the Lizano family since 1920. This one has obviously been perfected over the years and is very appealing. More steak sauce than hot sauce, it has some kick, but its primary merit is its complex flavor. I'd love to know what those vegetables are, but am happy nonetheless.

Miz Grazi's Hot Stuff Pepper Sauce

Michael's Enterprises, Inc. P.O. Box 400, Rosedale, MS 38769
■ 901-367-0888

Ingredients: Fresh red peppers, distilled vinegar, dehydrated onions, sugar, salt, garlic, spices, sodium benzoate

Comments: This sauce makes me want to take the first boat to Rosedale! From the day I was given a bottle of this special stuff, I've been in love with old Miz Grazi, even if she is a bit my senior. It's not particularly hot, but is packed with the flavor of Mississippi-grown red peppers. A touch of sugar to round things out, and a liberal dose of black pepper, make this the friend of everyone who enjoys grilling—hamburgers... steaks... chicken... vegie burgers... fish...

Mosquito Coast Pirate's Delight Swamp Bite Hot Sauce

Mosquito Coast Pirate's Delight Inc., 4644 Gandy Blvd., #7, Tampa, FL, 33611 ■ 813-837-8410

Ingredients: Sun-ripened tomatoes, the mighty habañero pepper, tropical peppers, salt, vinegar, herbs and spices

Comments: You won't be scratchin' when you're through with this one, but you will be itchin' for more. This is one of the best medium heat sauces I've tried. They don't mess around with a bunch of funkified ingredients to put out the fire. Rather, they put just the right amount of fire into each batch in the first place, and the result is a sauce with plenty of habañero flavor, without all the habañero heat. A good idea for those of you who haven't developed asbestos mouth yet, and a delicious change of pace for those who have.

Piri-Piri Mohlo Sauce

Domingos Ribeiro Macarico, Praia De Mira, Portugal

Ingredients: Piri piri pulp in brine

Comments: From across the Atlantic comes one of the ugliest-looking sauces in one of the ugliest bottles I've ever seen. Literally "Pepper-Pepper sauce," this ugly duckling is really a swan of flavor! If you can find this one, pick it up. It ought to be very cheap and very good, and it lends itself well to seafood.

Plaza Country-Style Pepper Sauce

Fletcher-Bowman Ltd., Yallahs, Jamaica, West Indies

Ingredients: Vinegar, papaya, chayote, cucumber, pepper, onion, mustard

Comments: This is a strange one indeed! No, chayote isn't a wild Jamaican dog; it most closely resembles squash, as near as I can tell. The cucumbers in this are great, and unusual as well. You will either love or hate this sauce, and that's about it. I like it a lot—try it for yourself.

Poblano Salsa Ranchera

Nicolas C. and Oscar R. Segura Inc., 648 West Lester Street, Tuscon, Arizona, 85705

Ingredients: Chili peppers, spices, distilled vinegar, salt, benzoate of soda

Comments: This is one of the best American sauces on the market and one that makes you wish you knew what the "spices" in the ingredients really are. Thick, and deep red in color, this sauce is loaded with delicious poblano flavor. Don't skip it because it's American—its roots are in Mexico and it tastes great!

Poblano Mexican Green Jalapeño Sauce

Nicolas C. and Oscar R. Segura and Company, 648 West Lester Street, Tuscon, Arizona, 85705

Ingredients: Green jalapeño peppers, spices, vinegar, salt, benzoate of soda

Comments: Another fine product from Nicolas and Oscar (a pair of unlikely names for purveyors of hot sauces), this one is as green as they get. It tastes mighty good—some care went into the growing of these jalapeños, as is evident from their depth of flavor. Maybe a little thin for some tastes, not hot enough for others, but still it's worth a shot, or two, or three...

Salsa Picante de la Viuda

Productos Sane De Chapala, S.A., Degollado 354 "A" Chapala, Jalisco, Mexico

Ingredients: Fresh red piquin peppers, vinegar, salt, spices, sodium benzoate

Comments: The widow ain't pretty, but she sure makes a good hot sauce. One thing is for sure—it wasn't this sauce that killed her husband, unless he got hit by the door as it was being knocked down for the recipe. It's a good one, done up in the traditional Mexican fashion, with fresh piquins giving it the kick that counts.

Shotgun Willie's Hot Sauce

Shotgun Willie's Place, Box 18868, Austin, Texas, 78760

Ingredients: Select aged cayenne, jalapeño, and tabasco peppers, distilled vinegar, salt, food stabilizer

Comments: "3-Barrel Hotter 'n Hell," they say. If hell were only this hot, there'd be a lot more sinnin' goin' on (and there's plenty as there is, thank goodness). It's an okay sauce, but if you've got a bottle of Backfire, you can save yourself a couple of bucks—this one's mighty similar.

Southern Country Gourmet Hot Sauce

Southern Country Inc., P.O. Box 4983, Monroe, Louisiana, 71211

Ingredients: Jalapeño peppers, cayenne peppers, vinegar, water, onions, sugar, salt, spices, sodium benzoate

Comments: This is reported to be a family recipe, passed down from generation to generation—if only our families had been so inventive! This is good stuff, kind of strange both in appearance and taste; the down side is that it can be a little expensive, but you can't take it with you anyway, so, go out with a bang.

Tamazula Salsa Picante

Salsa Tamazula, Calle 22 No. 2583, Zona Industrial,
Guadalajara, Jal., Mexico

Ingredients: Chili peppers, vinegar, salt, spices, sodium benzoate

Comments: This is a great example of the Mexican standard of hot sauces, something you might find in the average cupboard in Mexico. Not too hot, with a hint of fruit flavor, this sauce has a nice thickish consistency and a wonderful brownish red color.

Trappey's Chef Magic Jalapeño Sauce

B.F. Trappey's Sons, Inc., New Iberia, Louisiana, 70560

Ingredients: Purée of jalapeño peppers, distilled vinegar, salt, edible food stabilizer, F.D.& C. yellow #5

Comments: The Trappeys seem to have taken a cue or two from the McIlhenny boys on this one, or maybe the McIlhennys are actually making this one, who knows? Surprisingly spicy, with a tangy twist—not great, but worth having around to add some zip to your lip.

Tropical Ted's Rass Mon Gourmet Pepper Sauce

Hot Head Sauceworks, LLC., Rt. 1, Box 225-B, Deep Gap, North Carolina 28618 ■ 1-800-492-HOTR

Ingredients: Water, vinegar, honey, raisins, hot peppers, spices, lime juice, sugar, salt, soy sauce, garlic powder, onion powder

Comments: This is a great blend of flavors, Jamaican in style but straight out of North Carolina, where the local folks are known more for their independent nature than their hot-sauce production. This is surely an independent sauce, just hot enough to make you take notice, but not so hot that you can't make out the individual flavors that were stewed together so artfully. As the label attests, "Goodness Grows in North Carolina."

Westlow's Bonney Pepper Sauce

A product of Barbados, West Indies, imported and distributed by Louisiana-West Indies Trading Company, New Orleans, Louisiana, 70118

Ingredients: Ripe bonney peppers, onions, mustard flour, wheat flour, salt, sugar, turmeric, vinegar, sodium benzoate

Comments: You'll remember your old girlfriend Bonney as being a lot sweeter than this, but you'll love this versatile sauce all the same. Mustard yellow, this product is as lovely to look at as it is to eat. A complicated blend, uniquely thickened with two types of flour, and swimming in mild, flavorful peppers, this is one to add to your table.

Refrigeration?

Yes, and no. If it's a vinegar-based sauce with nothing odd in the mix (i.e., it has only vinegar, peppers, salt), no. Otherwise, it's generally a good idea to refrigerate all other sauces, especially selections with fruits, sugar, and, most poignantly, cider listed as ingredients.

Which leads to the next question: how am I supposed to fit all of these in the refrigerator? You have several options. You can give up beer and/or food, either one of which will free up a considerable amount of space. If you've got a basement or garage that isn't already filled with your collection of things that will surely come in handy one day, you can buy an old (and cheap) full-sized refrigerator; you'll be amazed how your hot-sauce collection will grow! Make sure the refrigerator works reasonably well, as you don't want to return from vacation to find 75 exploded bottles of habañero hell—now those gloves will really come in handy! Or—and this a reasonable option—buy a mini-refrigerator, (stake out a college dorm at the end of the school year, and buy one cheap when it won't fit into the family wagon) and learn to be satsified with the number of hot sauces it will hold.

Not That Good?

So you shelled out your hard earned money for this silly book and still bought a dud? Well, there's no accounting for taste, particularly my own, and this is bound to happen. Don't despair; think about how many pelts I've shelled out on ratty sauces so that I could attempt to steer you clear of most of the riffraff (yes, I am accepting cash donations, as my bank doesn't accept sympathy).

At any rate, you still have an option or two or three. You can put the lid back on it and give it to someone else, preferably someone you don't see very often, and who thinks you're an idiot anyway. Or you can get angry and throw it away.

Your best option, however, is to cook with it. It's amazing how a small amount of an otherwise disagreeable sauce can be transformed into interesting and hard to nail down flavors when added to your favorite dish. A small amount is the key here—relax, you'll get rid of it soon enough—or you'll end up with a larger version of what you didn't like in the first place, in which case it might be time to offer a neighborly gift to the newcomers down the street with the barking dogs and obnoxious yard art.

A Taste of Thai Garlic Chili Pepper Sauce

A product of Thailand; distributed in the U.S. by Andre Prost, Inc., P.O. Box AX, Old Saybrook, Connecticut, 06475

Ingredients: Red chile, water, sugar, garlic, vinegar, salt

Comments: If you're a garlic lover/chilehead, you can't do without this sauce. The seven-ounce bottle is widely available in America and is well worth whatever it costs, which usually isn't much. The combination of fiery hot Thai peppers and a healthy dose of fresh garlic will bring you back for more. Don't overdo—this is one of those sauces that sneaks up on you and clubs you over the tongue.

Big John's Famous Key West Really, Really Hot Sauce

Jones Productions, Box 362, Key West, Florida, 33041 ■ 305-296-1863

Ingredients: Red capsicums, Scotch bonnets, hot pickled carrots, vinegar, onions, garlic, spices

Comments: This is the only bottle of hot sauce I know of that is numbered by batch and individually hand signed by the creator. If this was my creation, I'd do the same; go to Key West if you have to, but find this sauce—it's that good! Big John advises using it on conch fritters, which is a great idea, but then again, I'd eat almost anything on conch fritters.

Bufalo Chipotle Sauce

A product of Mexico, distributed by Festin Food Corporation, Carlsbad, California, 92009

Ingredients: Water, vinegar, peppers, salt, sugar, artificial color, sodium benzoate, spices

Comments: What the folks at Bufalo miss with their jalapeño sauce, they make up for with this chipotle sauce: this stuff is smokey, spicy, and plenty thick—just like it should be. A generous portion makes this a good buy, too. Please, keep your editorial nit picking to yourself—this is how they spell buffalo!

Golden Delight Chunky Caribbean Hot Pepper Sauce

A product of Barbados, West Indies; distributed by Florida Dynamic Marketing Concept, Inc., 8382 N.W. 68th Street, Miami, Florida, 33166

Ingredients: Pepper, vinegar, mustard, onion, salt, sugar, spices

Comments: This is a widely available example of the mustard-based sauces of the West Indies. Golden yellow with chunks of red peppers floating about, this sunny-looking slather will heat you up on the coldest of days. This is a great mustard substitute, although a bit thin; leave the lid off for a few days to thicken it and concentrate the flavor a bit.

Hak Has Hot Pepper Sauce

Hak Has Manufacturing Limited, 62A Waterloo Road, Kingston 2, Jamaica, West Indies

Ingredients: Peppers, water, vinegar, sugar, salt, spices

Comments: The Hak Has sleeping half-moon label is a common sight on the island of Jamaica, where it graces tables in most eateries. It's a flavorful, slightly sweet blend of habañeros, some unknown but well-chosen spices, and plenty of Jamaican sunshine—a lethal combination, mon.

Hellfire & Damnation

A product of Belize, Central America; distributed by The El Paso Chile Company, 909 Texas Avenue, El Paso, Texas, 79901

Ingredients: Habañero peppers, fresh carrots, onions, garlic, fresh lime juice, vinegar, salt

Comments: Aptly named, Hellfire and Damnation will send your taste buds on a fiery journey to hell and back, at which point you'll surely damn yourself for the self-inflicted experience. The lime juice and salt endeavor to spread your palate wide open, and the habañeros rush in and do the job. Good stuff—always fresh.

Hot Buns at the Beach

Manufactured for Starboard Restaurant, 2009 Highway 1, Dewey Beach, Delaware, 19971 ■ 800-998-FIRE (call for a catalog)

Ingredients: Apple cider vinegar, a tremendous amount of habañero peppers, cayenne pepper mash, rica red peppers, ginger purée, even deeper well water, garlic juice, sweet potatoes, Barbados molasses, clear Shoyu, key lime juice, salt, a secret blend of natural herbs, flavors, and spices, and natural xanthan

Comments: This is one sauce I can slather on everything that dares to cross my plate. It's a bottle of really interesting sauce, with a depth of flavor not found everywhere. It's also plenty hot, hotter than any buns I've ever seen at the beach (actually, I'd rather ogle a bottle of hot sauce any day). This is also the only way you'll get me to eat sweet potatoes. Inhale enough of this sauce and you'll probably have hot buns of your own!

Island Heat Scotch Bonnet Pepper Sauce

A product of Jamaica, manufactured for Helen's Tropical-Exotics, Clarkston, Georgia, 30021

Ingredients: Papaya, Scotch bonnet peppers, tamarind, onions, vinegar, corn syrup, salt, tropical spices

Comments: This is a mild mannered Scotch bonnet (is that an oxymoron or what?) sauce, readily available in the United States. A bit too sweet for me, but perfectly acceptable if you like a little sugar with your spice.

Marin Products Salsa Picante de Chile Habañero

Felipe Marin Gonzalez, Calle 29, No. 182, Col. Miguel Aleman, Merida, Yucatan, Mexico, C.P. 97148 ■ Tel. 27-31-48

Ingredients: Habañero chile, tomato, vinegar, salt, spices, artificial colors, sodium benzoate

Comments: Señor Gonzalez offers us two fine products from his Marin hot sauce works. Both are habañero sauces, one green and one red. The green sauce takes advantage of an early harvest and is somewhat milder than other habañero sauces but has a delicious fresh flavor. The red sauce is blended from habañeros picked at their prime and maintains a heftier heat, with a somewhat musty flavor. These are both excellent sauces and are reputed to gain heat as they age.

Melinda's Amarillo Hot Mustard Pepper Sauce

Produced in Costa Rica for Melinda's Gourmet Food Products, 722 Martin Behrman Avenue, Metarie, LA 70005 ■ 800-886-6354

Ingredients: Fresh onion, habañero peppers, food starch, mustard, sugar, salt, vinegar, flour, turmeric, sodium benzoate

Comments: This is a great product from the wickedly inventive kitchen of Melinda. As the color would indicate, this sauce is dominated by a first-rate mustard flavor but sizzles with habañeros as well. What sets this sauce apart from the other mustard-based sauces is its consistency—as thick as the come-on lines at a singles' bar on Saturday night—but much more palatable. This texture gives the sauce versatility, making it a perfect companion to your grilled foods; you'll find it particularly well suited to shrimp.

Mrs. Dog's Dangerously Hot Pepper Sauce

Mrs. Dog's Products, Inc., P.O. Box 6034, Grand Rapids, Michigan, 49516
■ 616-940-1778

Ingredients: Hot Portugal peppers, habañero peppers, allspice, vinegar, salt, sorbic acid

Comments: First things first: as an owner of many mangy beasts, I can assure you that your dog isn't going to like this sauce. You, on the other hand, will probably find yourself quite fond of it, even if it won't fetch the morning paper or get you another beer. This might be the mildest habañero sauce I've tried, but it's still worth a try as the addition of allspice gives it a unique flavor, and makes this dog no Heinz 57.

Travelin' with Tabasco

The Tabasco label is an internationally recognized icon, and thus allows unencumbered passage through most foreign customs offices. Tabasco sauce is also, in my humble and admittedly biased opinion, the sauce to choose if you can choose only one. Most of this has to do with its no-nonsense flavor and its medium to hot intensity; Tabasco doesn't overpower anything and won't insult most cooks. Perhaps more important, the next day it won't leave you searching for toilet paper in the Gobi Desert.

The two-ounce size is nicely portable and will outlast all but the most extended vacations. (If you're traveling in a group, urge your friends to bring a bottle or two in order to avoid the dreaded last drops scenario of "it was such a great idea to bring this, do you mind if I finish it off?") Beyond this, the bottle is reasonably tough, with a good sturdy cap that won't leak during transport.

Endorphin High

Feeling pleasantly light-headed after a particularly spicy meal? It's probably the work of endorphins. According to my dictionary, an endorphin is "any of a group of peptide hormones that bind to opiate receptors and are found mainly in the brain." The key word here is "opiate;" endorphins can definitely create some short-lived bliss, as short as five minutes or as long as fifteen.

Endorphins are released by your brain after you eat fiery foods. I'm not going to explain why—just enjoy the sensation. The only other way to experience this rush is to jog until your shoes fall off, an activity I avoid at all costs.

Funky Ingredients

Wondering what some of those things are that you see listed in the ingredients on your latest purchase of hot sauce? Sodium benzoate? Edible food stabilizer (was it unstable earlier)? Xanthan gum (for blowing bubbles)? What is all this stuff? Quite simply, they are additives that serve to enhance flavor, preserve the other ingredients, or prevent them from changing into something, presumably, that no one would be safe (or at least happy) eating.

These ingredients are perhaps even more numerous and varied than the peppers used to make hot sauces, and whether or not you want to ingest them is as individual a decision as choosing underwear. Do your own thing and live (or die from) the consequences. I'm alive after a quarter of a century of swallowing these various goops—check back in another 25, if you're really concerned.

911 Hot Sauce

Sanctuary Much, Inc., Morton Grove, Illinois, 60053 ■ 708-470-9112

Ingredients: Onions, water, Scotch bonnet peppers, vinegar, bell peppers, prepared mustard, canola oil, mango purée, lime juice, salt, spices, black pepper, lecithin, xantham gum, sodium benzoate, sodium metabisulfite

Comments: While this sauce probably won't cause you to dial your local 911 operator, it might encourage you to call these folks in Illinois and say, "Sanctuary Much!!" This is one of the most flavorful sauces out there, enhanced by a very tasty dash of mustard. Not tremendously hot, but it will "elevate your enjoyment of food by a few degrees" and might just alter your perspective on the cornfields of Illinois.

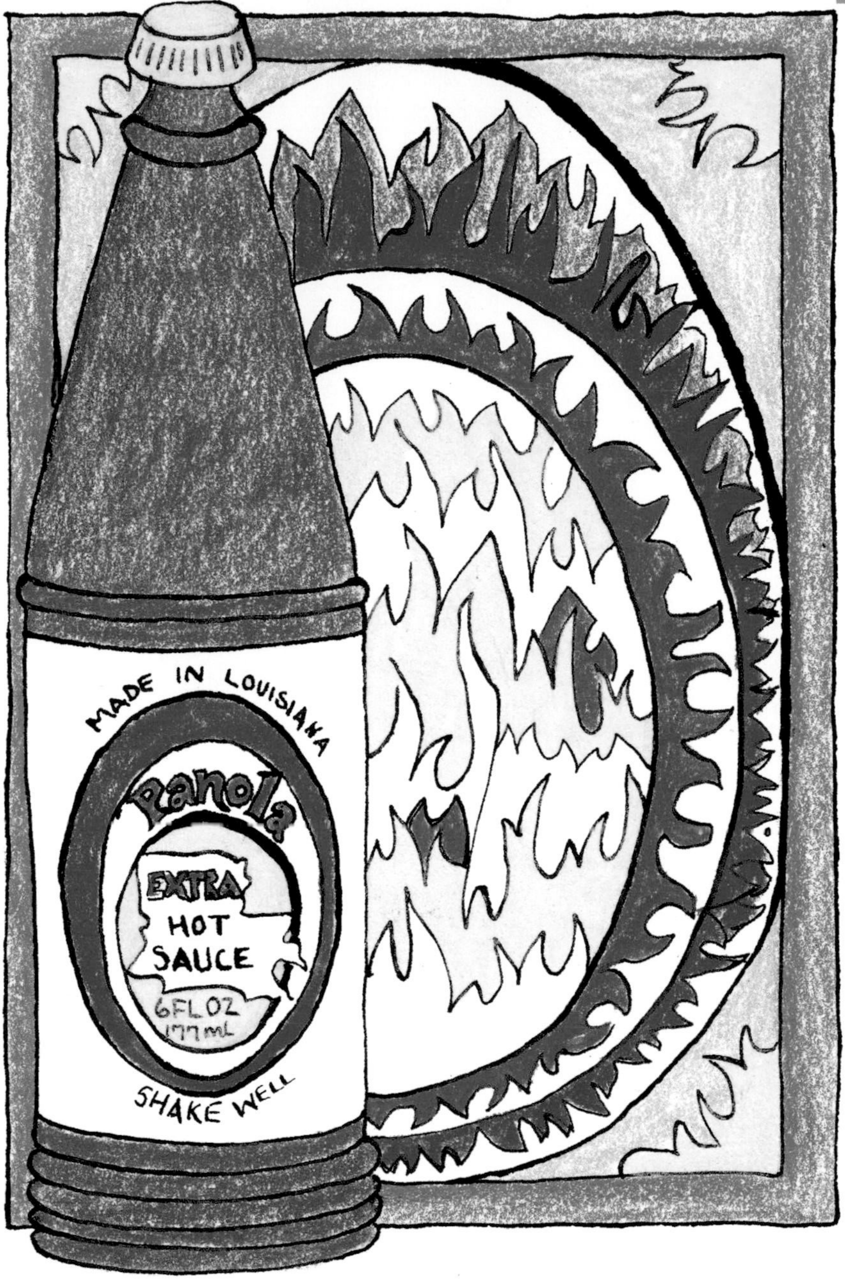

Panola Extra Hot Sauce

Panola Pepper Corporation, Rt. 2, Box 148, Lake Providence, Louisiana, 71254 ■ 318-559-1774

Ingredients: Aged pepper mash, vinegar, salt, cellulose gum, certified food color

Comments: Panola has for decades been turning out some of Louisiana's finest sauces, and this is no exception. In fact, this may be the company's best offering; it is certainly the hottest Panola has to offer. Don't be fooled by its pale red color and thin consistency—this is plenty hot and plenty good—I guarantee!!

Ramson's Hot Pepper Sauce

Chas. E. Ramson Limited, 449 Spanish Town Road, Kingston 11, Jamaica, West Indies

Ingredients: Peppers, vinegar, sugar, salt, water, spices, preservative

Comments: Yet another barn burner from the island of Jamaica—how much hot can there be on one island?!? A lot, evidently, as this red sauce packs plenty of punch, along with the deliciously distinct flavor of habañero peppers and those ubiquitous "spices." You'll find yourself longing for a cold tropical drink before you're through with this one. A five-ounce supply will go a long way, if you can find it.

Salsa Picante de Chile de Arbol

From the Kitchens of Montezuma

Sauces and Salsas, Ltd., 7856 Forest Brook Ct., Powell, Ohio, 43065

Ingredients: Chile de arbol, chile guajillo, water, cider vinegar, pumpkin seeds, sesame seeds, fresh garlic, spices, salt

Comments: This is one of the most imaginative sauces on the market, and also one of the best. Montezuma gets his revenge here, combining two hot peppers, the arbol and the guajillo, to create a salsa that is nicely balanced out with pumpkin and sesame seeds, not to mention a nice touch of garlic. Hot, but sophisticated—I suggest you buy it.

Scorned Woman Hot Sauce

Oak Hill Farms, P.O. Box 888302, Atlanta, Georgia, 30356

Ingredients: Tabasco peppers, habañero peppers, vinegar, lemon juice, green chile peppers, black pepper, salt, xantham gum

Comments: Whoever was the first to scorn this woman was surely made to pay with his stomach lining, and this sauce takes the same path. A reasonable heat index and a nice touch of lemon make this bottle stand out from the crowd. Maybe just a smidgen too much black pepper for some, but a great sauce nonetheless. Keep scornin' her!

Sriracha Hot Chili Sauce

Huy Fong Foods, Inc., 5001 Earle Avenue, Rosemead, California, 91770
■ 818-286-8328

Ingredients: Chili, distilled vinegar, garlic, salt, sugar, potassium sorbate, sodium bisulfite

Comments: In addition to being a first-rate hot sauce, this is a true bargain—17 ounces for generally next to nothing. Plenty of heat, with a great garlic accent, and the squirt bottle really lets you slather it on with ease. They recommend using it in soup, which, for those of you who don't do it already, is a great use for most hot sauces.

Tabasco Pepper Sauce

As-if-you-didn't-know, Avery Island, Louisiana, 70513

Ingredients: Vinegar, red peppers, salt

Comments: This is the most common and sometimes the most overlooked sauce in America. Kind of like an old car—with so many new products around, why try this old clunker? Well, because new doesn't always mean better, and this sauce is damned good, always has been, always will be. There is no better sauce to cook with, and small amounts add the secret ingredient to a myriad of dishes, from crawfish pie to apple pie. Take it everywhere you go. Put one in your tackle box. As if this isn't reason enough, the McIlhenny family are truly a great bunch of folks, and if anyone deserves your business, they do. Buy it by the gallon!!

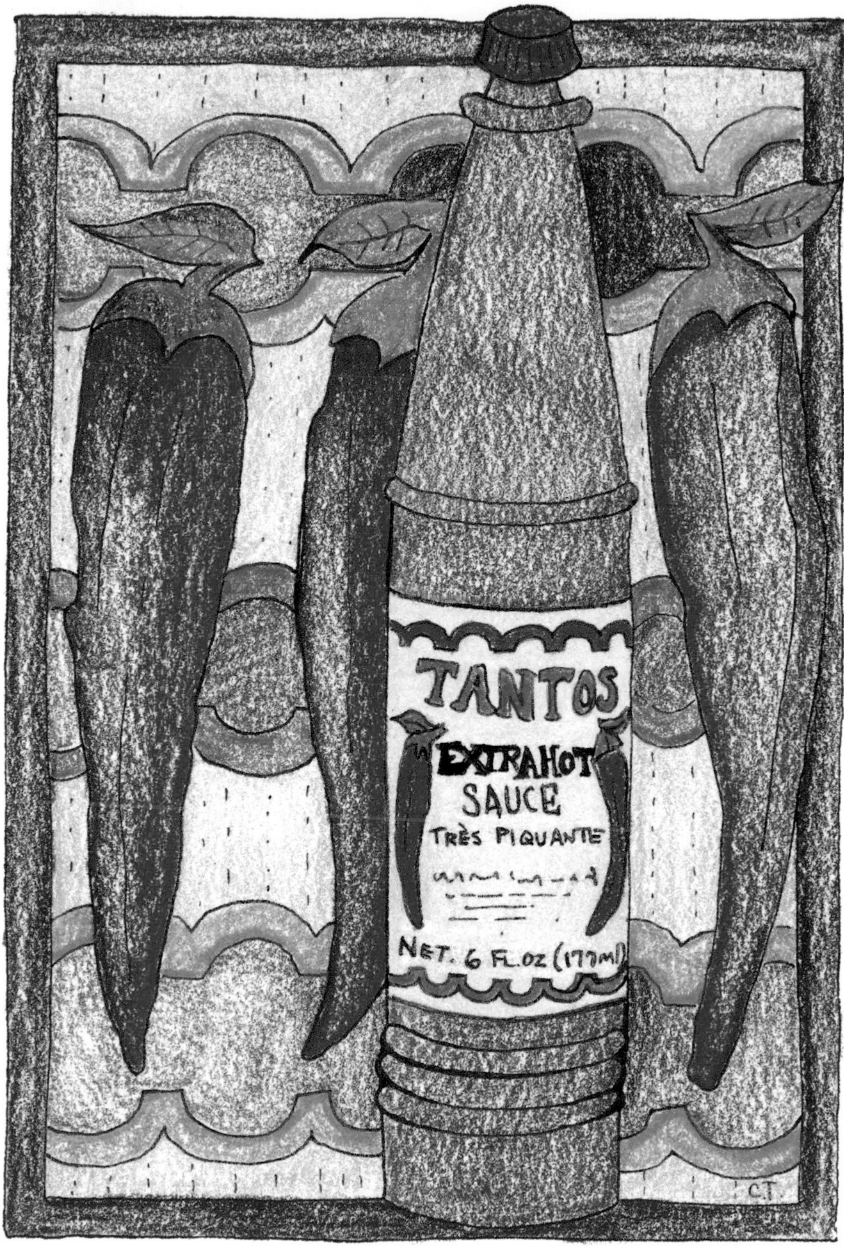

Tantos Extra Hot Sauce

A product of Costa Rica, Central America, imported by Noors' Import, Canada ■ FAX 416-731-5881

Ingredients: Cayenne pepper, vinegar, salt, spices, xantham gum

Comments: One thing is for sure—the Costa Ricans don't care much for fancy labels or fancy names; what they do care about is hot sauce. And they do mean hot. Très piquante!! Bursting with cayenne flavor that takes a licking and keeps on kicking. Get some.

Uncle Al's Old Fashioned Hot Sauce

Maw Pepper Productions, Montego Bay, Jamaica, West Indies

Ingredients: Pepper, vinegar, salt, sugar, pawpaw, pimento, spices

Comments: Uncle Al's been out in the pawpaw patch again, and what he brought back tastes more like habañero than a relative of the custard-apple family. Pawpaw is a staple of Montego Bay, where Jamaicans know hot food, and how. This sauce is hard to find—you may have to (have to?!?) go to Jamaica to obtain it. If you do, pick up a bottle or two. Uncle Al will be glad you did, and so will you and your friends.

Author's Top Twelve

I'm sometimes asked, if you had to choose one... Choose one? Not possible. However, thanking our forefathers for not opting for communism, I am able to narrow things down to an even dozen.

ON THE MILD SIDE

Cajun Chef Brand Green Hot Sauce

Hammond's Jamaica Style Hot Pepper Sauce

Miz Grazi's Hot Pepper Sauce

Texas Pete

WARMING TREND

Big John's Famous Key West Really, Really Hot Sauce

Mosquito Coast Pirate's Delight Swamp Bite Hot Sauce

Tabasco Pepper Sauce

Vampire Hot Sauce

BOILING OVER

Island Spice Dragon Pepper Sauce

Miss Anna's Hot Pepper Sauce

Salsa's Smoked Habañero Salsa

Spicy Hot Pepper Sauce from the Pork Pit

Squirrels in Your Feeder

Squirrels in our bird feeders drive me batty. I've tried everything to deter them; my wife has forbidden the local hardware stores to sell me a pellet gun, more in deference to our neighbors' windows than to the squirrels' well-being.

So, from my mother-in-law, master gardener and squirrel abater extraordinaire, comes this solution: mix dried ground pepper in with your bird seed. It works, most of the time. According to her research, conducted in her backyard lab, 80 percent of the squirrels have an adverse reaction to the pepper dusting, while less than one percent of the birds shy away from the mix. I don't have my abacus handy to figure this out exactly, but I can tell you that since adopting this practice we see a lot more birds than squirrels in our feeders.

One word of advice: don't spend the beans on small "Squirrel Be Gone" type packets at your local aviary shop; buy bulk cayenne pepper at your grocery store—it's the same thing at a fraction of the price. Then, sit back, relax, and let the fireworks begin!

Bello Hot Pepper Sauce

Parry W. Bellot & Company, Ltd., Castle Comfort, Dominica

Ingredients: Scotch bonnet peppers, papaya, onion, vinegar, salt, spices

Comments: If Castle Comfort has a moat, you might want to jump in and cool off after taking a swig of this. From the land of black sand beaches (honestly, check it out for yourself) and crystal clear waters, Bello is blistering hot and utterly enjoyable, with just enough papaya to keep things in check. Keep it away from the kids and all of your wimpy friends.

Community Kitchens Ville Platte Hot Sauce

Community Coffee Company, P.O. Box 3778, Baton Rouge, Louisiana, 70821 ■ 800-535-9901

Ingredients: Vinegar, salt, peppers

Comments: This sauce is one of my all-time favorites—simple in the tradition of tabasco pepper sauces, yet somehow complex beyond its ingredients. Ville Platte is proof that it's the peppers that count: no mumbo gumbo here, just straight up, knock your socks off, run home crying hot sauce. Put their 800 number on your speed dialer.

El Yucateco Salsa Popular de Chile Habañero
(Red or Green)

Produced and packed by Priamo J. Gamboa, Merida, Yucatan, Mexico

Ingredients: Habañero peppers, vinegar, iodated salt, garlic, spices

Comments: These are two of the best Mexican sauces I've tried, and I highly recommend both the red and the green. As inexpensive as most Mexican sauces, these two won't just pick you up: they'll pick you up and throw you down. Genuine habañero fire—take this pair seriously.

Geddy's Hot Pepper Sauce

Packed in Jamaica for T. Geddes Ltd., 109 Marcus Garvey Drive, Kingston, Jamaica, West Indies

Ingredients: Capsicums, vinegar, water, sugar, salt, spices, approved preservatives

Comments: Another of the make-your-hair-stand-on-end table sauces from our friends in Jamaica. This is a very desirable sauce, as it's very delicious, very hot, and very hard to find off the island of Jamaica (hint, hint—somebody import this, please!). As a matter of fact, I stole (procured?) my bottle from the Sandals Resort in Montego Bay—they had plenty, and I didn't!! Find it if you can.

Grace Original Jamaican Hot Pepper Sauce

Grace, Kennedy, and Company, Limited, 64 Harbour Street, Kingston, Jamaica, West Indies

Ingredients: Capsicum pepper, water, cane vinegar, salt, sugar

Comments: They say that if it's bottled or canned on the island of Jamaica, Grace did it; and what they've bottled here will knock you on your can if you're not careful. This sauce is THE standard table sauce in Jamaica. A great, straight-up habañero sauce, it's not to be messed with in large quantities or with groups of crybabies. Jamaicans like it hot, and you'll like this.

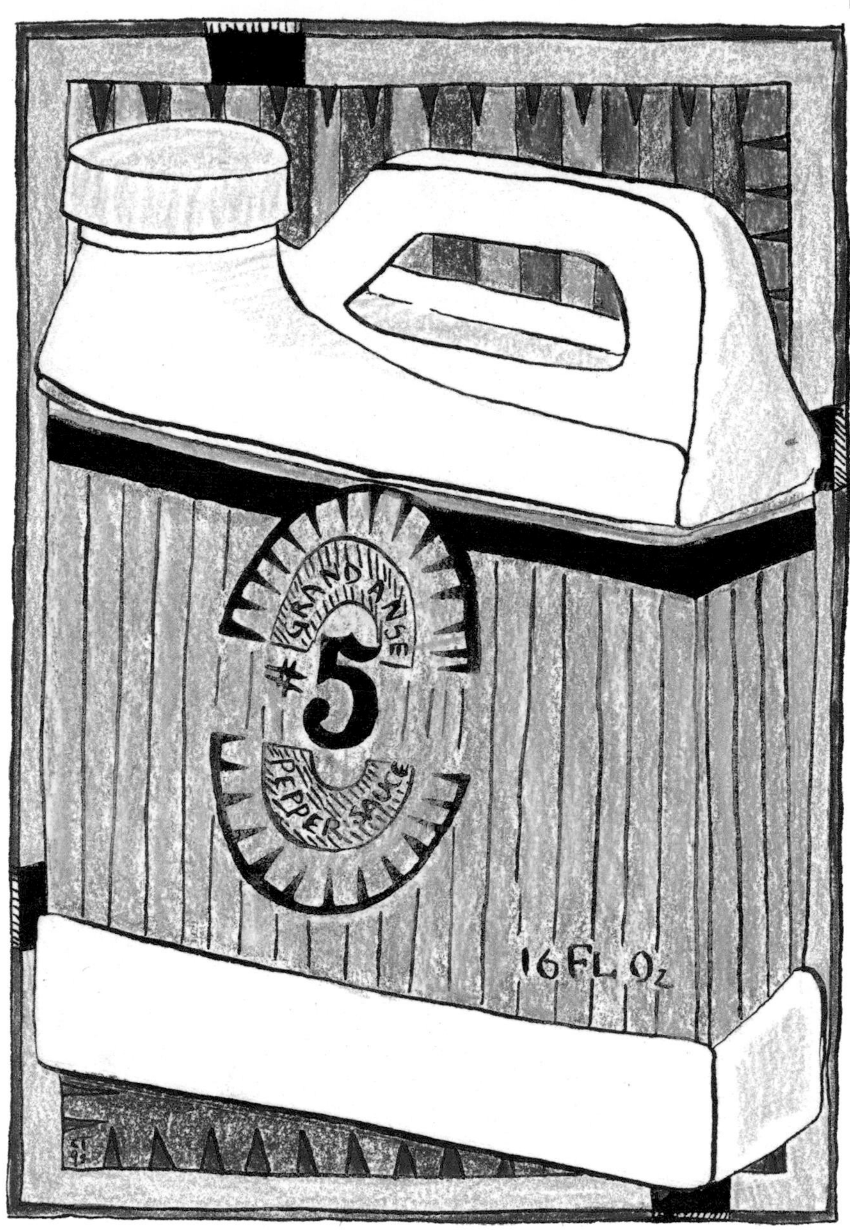

Grand Anse #5 Pepper Sauce

A product of Grenada, West Indies; distributed by American West India Trading Company, P.O. Box 1083, Cincinnati, Ohio, 45201

Ingredients: Scotch bonnet peppers, vinegar, mustard, corn starch, onions, salt, garlic, sodium benzoate

Comments: Said to be a family recipe passed down over generations, this is one outstanding hot sauce, even if its pasty yellowish complexion isn't the most attractive on the shelf. It's available in a two-ounce bottle and a 16-ounce jug, so get both—you'll want lots, and you'll be socially responsible by refilling the small container instead of throwing it out. Hot? Yes! Flavor? Lots!!

Grand Anse Obeah Pepper Oil

A product of the U.S. Virgin Islands, distributed by American West India Trading Company, P.O. Box 1083, Cincinnati, Ohio, 45201

Ingredients: Peanut oil, steeped in Scotch bonnet peppers

Comments: Okay, so technically it's not a hot sauce: but it's very hot, and you can pour it—so there you have it. This is a great substitute any time you cook with SMALL quantities of oil. The label says that "Fire is the weapon of the voodoo spirit Obeah." I don't know anything about voodoo, but I do know that this stuff Obeah hot!!!

Gloves?

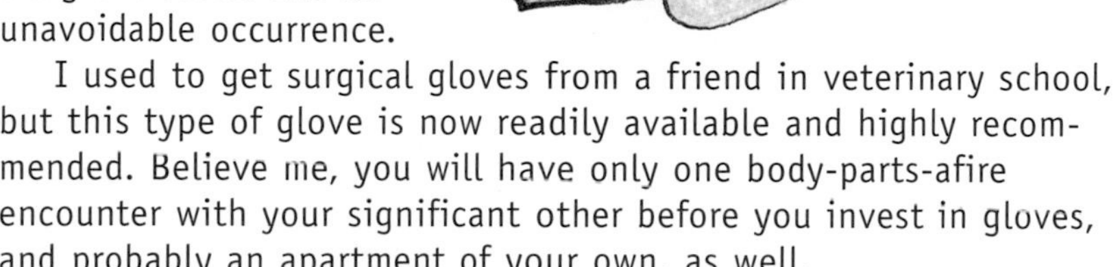

Yes, if you value your goods, or are a closet nose picker. Years ago, thick and clumsy dish-washing gloves were the only option when handling hot, raw peppers, and slicing your fingers while trimming the stems was an unavoidable occurrence.

I used to get surgical gloves from a friend in veterinary school, but this type of glove is now readily available and highly recommended. Believe me, you will have only one body-parts-afire encounter with your significant other before you invest in gloves, and probably an apartment of your own, as well.

By the way, if you choose to ignore my well-intentioned advice, Jean Andrews suggests in her book, *Peppers, The Domesticated Capsicums*, that you soak your hands in a solution of bleach and water. Why not just get the gloves?

Rare Opportunities

Some of the hot elixirs mentioned in this book will probably never be found in the U.S. Although this can be frustrating, it can also be fun. Here are three proven tactics for obtaining them.

1. If you can't find a certain sauce, having pestered every merchant in a 60-mile radius, give the manufacturer a call. A few will definitely tell you to shove off—big deal, nothing ventured, nothing gained. Others will be happy to sell you some, but you may have to buy a case: perfect—if you really want it, surely lots of your friends will as well and you'll soon recoup your investment, or worst case, be sitting on a great bunch of holiday gifts. If a manufacturer won't ship it to you because you don't have a food service permit or don't conform to some other stupid rule, talk to friends who own a restaurant, store, or bait shop—the hot sauce maker will have no reason not to ship it to them.

2. Keep track of where these manufacturers brew their sauces, and if you're heading in the general direction, make a quick side trip, buy some sauce, probably get a tour.

3. Take advantage of people who travel, particularly those who travel outside the United States. Got a friend going to St. Croix? Ask them to pick up a few bottles of Miss Anna's. Simple as that, with one tiny trick: you must part with at least a twenty dollar bill. Even your best friend won't remember that you gave him five bucks for hot sauce until he's spending it on an overpriced drink on the flight home. A twenty, though, will lube the memory, and most likely you'll get your treasured sauce.

Island Spice Dragon Pepper Sauce

Island Spice Limited, 2 South Camp Road, Kingston C.S.O., Jamaica, West Indies ■ 809-928-9217

Ingredients: A delectable mess of great peppers

Comments: I ran across this one in a strip mall outside of Montego Bay, and the only reason I bought it was the “buy something or get lost” look I was getting from the proprietor. I couldn’t be happier that he gave me the evil eye, as he unknowingly steered me toward a fantastic bottle of hot sauce. It’s spicy enough to make you take notice (and run for cover) but more flavorful than any other Jamaican table sauce I’ve tried, with the perfect amount of salt. I haven’t seen it here—yet another in your long list of reasons to go to the islands.

Last Rites

Hot Heads, Inc., 3307 Kissel Hill Road, Lititz, Pennsylvania, 17543

Ingredients: Scotch bonnet peppers, vinegar, water, natural spices, salt, citric acid, xantham gum

Comments: Not the most flavorful sauce in the cupboard, but hot as Hades!!! The label says that it "will take the rust off your car, and give you ten more miles to the gallon!" Not to mention knocking you out of your rocking chair and scalding your cat! Administer this at your next opportunity.

Los Chileros Jamaican Fire Scotch Bonnet Salsa

Imported and marketed in the U.S. by Los Chileros De Nuevo Mexico, P.O. Box 6215, Santa Fe, New Mexico, 87502 505-471-6967 ■ FAX 473-7306

Ingredients: Water, Scotch bonnet peppers, vinegar, modified food starch, salt, approved spices, sodium benzoate, sodium bisulfite

Comments: This is your basic, nothing fancy, no frills bottle of pure hell. What little water there is in each bottle is smothered by Scotch bonnets, as will be your taste buds. For the purist in all of us—highly recommended.

Roberts Hot Pepper Sauce

Roberts Products Company, Ltd., 7 Norwich Avenue, Kingston 11, Jamaica, West Indies

Ingredients: Hot peppers, vinegar, sugar, salt, spices

Comments: I once met a man in Jamaica named Robert who claimed to be a fire-breathing dragon; he could be the genie in this bottle. When it comes to hot sauce, Jamaicans are cruel, and this innocent looking bottle is proof positive of this notion. The Jamaicans lay this stuff on thick—you better take it easy, mon!!

Salsa's Smoked Habañero Salsa

Salsa Mexican-Caribbean Cuisine, 6 Patton Avenue, Asheville, North Carolina ■ 704-252-9805

Ingredients: Hector (the inimitable owner of Salsa) ain't talkin'! Not on this subject, anyway.

Comments: Admittedly, I'm completely biased on this one, which is from my favorite restaurant, (among restaurants that make their own hot sauce—yes, I'm hedging) which also happens to be in the town where I live, and about two blocks from where I work. Having said that, I would love this sauce if it came from Mars. It is the smokiest of the hottest and the hottest of the smokiest, and it's typical of Hector's on-the-edge but not over-the-edge cooking style. This sauce will light you up to the point of perfection, causing discomfort only in the case of overindulgence, which can't exactly be blamed on Hector—hey, we're all grown ups, aren't we? Make a pilgrimage to Asheville and camp out at Salsa; be careful though—you might never want to leave.

Floating Chiles

A great addition to any kitchen is a bottle of olive oil or vinegar infused with the flavor and heat of chiles. Select your favorite hot peppers in a size that will squeeze through the bottle neck (see, I am the brains of this operation!), blanch them slightly in vinegar or oil, depending on the direction you're heading, and slit the sides of the peppers (you are wearing gloves, right?) to allow for maximum soakage. Then simply fill up the bottles with peppers and oil or peppers and vinegar.

The more attractive the bottles the better, as you'll want this stuff displayed on your countertop—it really is a beautiful sight. For extra zest, add several peeled cloves of garlic. Mix the infused oil and vinegar together for an eye-popping salad dressing.

Long and Hot, Short and Hotter

No, this isn't my latest idea for a food vending cart, an endorsement for the virility of short men, or a description of my last two summers. It's the difference between jalapeños and habañeros.

I'll admit it, jalapeños kill me for hours. They have this agonizingly brain numbing effect of inducing me into eating a dozen or so, pickled, whole, with a tray of cheese, only to remind me of why I swore I would never do this again: the heat lasts forever, and then some.

Habañeros, on the other hand, send me into orbit in a very different manner: smokin', chokin', rollin' in the yard, praying for mercy, speaking in tongues, it ain't never gonna end...hey, what happened? The burn is gone! Habañeros, for all their savage heat, are the most merciful peppers on the planet. So, pick your poison, and don't say I didn't warn you.

Sontava! Habañero Pepper Hot Sauce

A product of Belize, Central America, imported by Jardine and McIntosh Trading Company, P.O. Box 18868, Austin, Texas, 78760 ■ 800-544-1880

Ingredients: Choice red habañero peppers, fresh carrots, onions, lime juice, vinegar, garlic, salt, and nothing else!

Comments: A familiar recipe out of Belize, this one claims to be the original habañero pepper hot sauce. I don't know whether or not this is true, but I do know that this sauce is "Some Kind of Wonderful." Very spicy and very flavorful (I have a weak spot for carrots!), this is one of the sauces to be stranded on a desert island with, provided the island has plenty of refreshments to drink. The label says that "Sontava" was the first sound used to describe this sauce, and thus the name. "Aaah!"—was all I had to say. This is a must-have sauce and easy to find.

Vampfire Hot Sauce

Panola Pepper Corporation, Rt. 2 Box 148, Lake Providence, Louisiana, 71254 ■ 318-559-1774

Ingredients: Habañero peppers, tabasco peppers, cayenne peppers, distilled vinegar, onions, sugar, salt, spices, lemon oil, cellulose gum, certified food coloring

Ingredients: I thought this sauce was a gimmick when I saw it in the store around Halloween; then I looked at the ingredients and knew that this bottle meant business. This is the only Louisiana sauce that I know of that uses habañeros, and the first three ingredients read like a Who's Who of Hot. They say it's made up the road from Transylvania, Lousiana, and like any vampire, it's got some teeth. Call Panola if you can't find this sauce in the store, or wait for it to appear around Halloween.

Walker's Wood Hot Jamaican Jonkanoo Pepper Sauce

Cottage Industries Limited, Walkerswood P.O., St. Ann, Jamaica, West Indies ■ 800-827-0769

Ingredients: Hot peppers, water, scallion, vinegar, citric acid, thyme, onion, salt, sugar, garlic, corn starch, sodium benzoate

Comments: One glance at the list of ingredients, and I knew this was a good bet—the attractive bottle was a plus as well. This is one of my favorite sauces, a blend of blazing hot peppers with subtle seasonings—the combination of which is out of this world. Jonkanoo? Who knows—all the Jamaicans I asked just smiled in the way only Jamaicans can smile and ambled on down the road.

Chugging Beer to Cool the Fire

While I regard chugging beer as a reasonably good idea in general, it's really not such a great idea in this case. Becoming inebriated to the point of gastronomical expulsion while enjoying a hot-sauce feast is a monumentally dim-witted notion, as anyone who has experienced it will attest, and I'm certainly not confessing here, Mom.

More to the point is that beer, water, juice, and all other water-based drinks simply will not aid your flaming molars. Dairy products are the key: milk, sour cream, yogurt, and, best of all, ice cream.

What is causing you to hop around on one foot and scream is oil-borne and won't be remedied with watery solutions. Dairy products, however, will whisk away your misery, leaving you ready, willing, and able to inflict more pain upon yourself. I once read that dogs have no memory for pain—surely they meant chileheads.

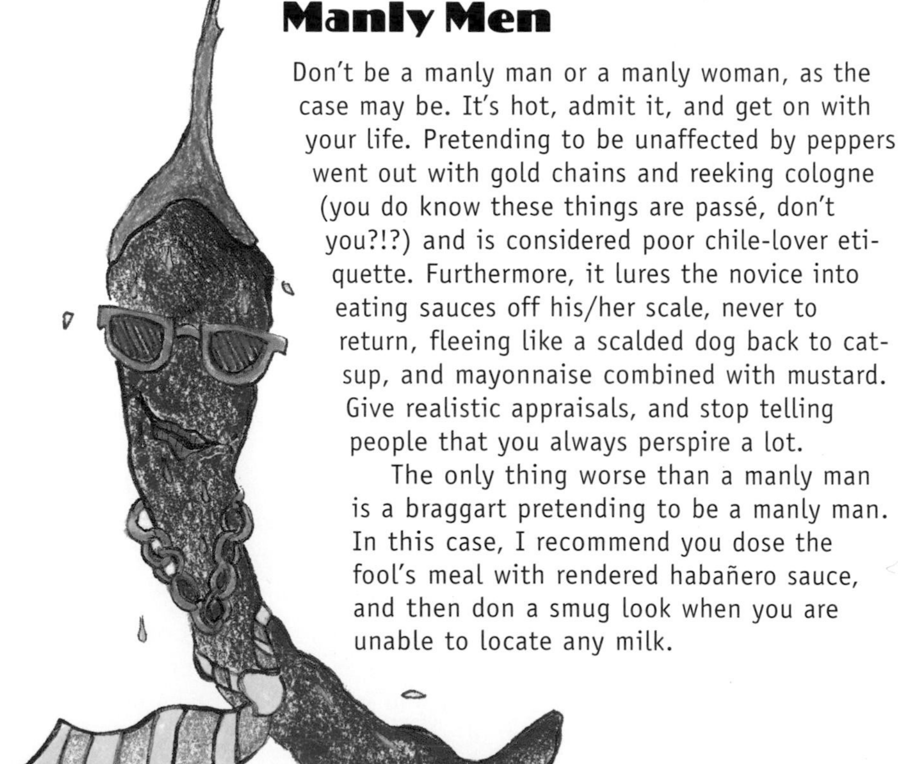

Manly Men

Don't be a manly man or a manly woman, as the case may be. It's hot, admit it, and get on with your life. Pretending to be unaffected by peppers went out with gold chains and reeking cologne (you do know these things are passé, don't you?!?) and is considered poor chile-lover etiquette. Furthermore, it lures the novice into eating sauces off his/her scale, never to return, fleeing like a scalded dog back to catsup, and mayonnaise combined with mustard. Give realistic appraisals, and stop telling people that you always perspire a lot.

The only thing worse than a manly man is a braggart pretending to be a manly man. In this case, I recommend you dose the fool's meal with rendered habañero sauce, and then don a smug look when you are unable to locate any milk.

Dave's Gourmet Insanity Sauce

Manufactured for Dave's Gourmet, Inc., 108 North Columbus Street, Alexandria, VA, 22314

Ingredients: Tomato sauce, onions, hot pepper extract, chili peppers, water, soy oil, vinegar, garlic salt, xantham gum, spices

Comments: Billed as "The Hottest Sauce In The Universe," this is one sauce that lives up to its bragging. The rather innocuous ingredient list disguises the beast within; have a big glass of milk or a pint of ice cream ready, as this sauce will blast you into another realm of culinary torture. The wicked inclusion of soy oil makes this stuff linger until you've had enough and are ready to go home and lick your wounds. The folks at Dave's Gourmet warn you to use it one drop at a time, and this is a warning well heeded.

Jamaica Hell Fire Hot Pepper Concentrate

Manufactured by Dr. Duphorn, Johnston, & Company, 4625, North Manhattan Avenue, Suite J, Tampa, Florida, 33614, under license from Dr. Duphorn, Johnston, & Company, Ltd., P.O. Box 22, Gordon Town P.O., St Andrew, Jamaica, West Indies

Ingredients: Sun-ripened tropical hot peppers, Blue Mountain pimento, vinegar, salt, sorbic acid

Comments: Dr. Duphorn has been out in the Jamaican sun too long, and it has boiled his brain. As a result, he'll boil yours with this cruel and unusual sauce. He advises that "to prepare hot pepper sauce of 'normal' strength, dilute one part Jamaica Hell Fire with two parts of water and one part of vinegar." No way! Brace yourself, quit complaining, and take a swig. Then head for the horse trough!

Miss Anna's Hot Pepper Sauce

Somewhere on St. Croix, U.S. Virgin Islands

Ingredients: Pepper, water, vinegar, mustard, onion, garlic, curry, salt

Comments: Simply put, my absolute favorite and a big surprise, too. Relaxing at a neighborhood dive on St. John, I liberally doused my conch fritters with Miss Anna's, and went into orbit! This sauce is scorchingly hot! But it's so full of flavor that I couldn't help myself. I soon became the amusement of the hour for the natives who gathered to observe my escalating problem. Curry and garlic, the distractions from the habañero heat, meld together nicely with a hearty helping of onions and mustard. I only wish I had purchased more, as I've never seen this in the United States—guess I'll have to go back!

MP West Indian Hot Flambeau Sauce

National Canneries Limited, C.R. Highway, Arima, Trinidad, West Indies

Ingredients: Hot peppers, onions, salt, mustard, food starch, white vinegar, garlic

Comments: If you buy a bottle of this, and I truly hope you do, be warned: what looks like a bottle of ketchup is most certainly not. This is one of the hottest sauces around, and you must warn your family and friends before setting it on the refrigerator shelf. (Unless you enjoy inflicting terribly cruel jokes on those you love.) HOT! HOT! HOT!

Spicy Hot Pepper Sauce from The Pork Pit

The Pork Pit, Montego Bay, Jamaica, West Indies

Ingredients: Secret, but HOT!!

Comments: There is only one way to get this sauce, and once you've had it, you may wish you hadn't. Fly to Jamaica, get a cab (say your prayers; Jamaicans are very mellow until they get behind the wheel) and say two words—"Pork Pit." The driver will know the way; if not, it's up the beach on the left in downtown Montego Bay. Order food and plenty to drink from the outside bar and restaurant; cautiously season your food with the sauce on the counter; sit, eat—and catch on fire. Ah, heaven! (The "festival" bread will help quiet your screaming taste buds, but not much.) The Pork Pit has probably the best Jerk food on the planet, and their sauce is without equal. Go there. Get some. No problem!

Stonewall Chili Pepper Company Salsa Habañero

Stonewall Chili Pepper Company, Highway 290, Box 241,
Stonewall, Texas, 78671

Ingredients: Chili habañeros, fresh lime juice, vinegar, sea salt, garlic

Comments: This is the rocket fuel that, on one fateful New Year's day, reduced one serious chilehead I know to tears. After tasting this sauce on a toothpick (!), he ran about our house begging, pleading, demanding a glass of milk. We had none and thus were obligated to prolong his misery, and our amusement. This is serious stuff—have some milk ready.

West Indies Creole Hot Pepper Sauce

P.W. Bellot & Co., Ltd., Castle Comfort, Dominica, West Indies

Ingredients: Peppers, papaya, onions, salt, vinegar, spices

Comments: This little brown jug of fire is enough to set off even the most hardened of palates. A thick brownish red habañero concoction, nicely balanced with papaya and a hint of onion, this ten-ounce bottle is likely to last a lifetime, unless you've got a stomach of steel and a taste for pain.

Would You Care to See the Wine List?

My father-in-law, whose knowledge of wine is surpassed only by his knowledge of the University of South Carolina's football team, is wont to tell me that my palate has been seared beyond comprehension. There is some credence to this theory. Consequently, I don't recommend spending 20 to 30 dollars on a bottle of wine to accompany chile rellenos garnished with roasted Scotch bonnets, or, for that matter, attempting any complex wine with spicy food. The spicy food will win (all right!!), and you would have been better off spending your money on more hot sauce.

However, wine and hot sauce are by no means mutually exclusive (my father-in-law's blood pressure just went off the scale!). The most obvious choice would be a hearty red wine, not unlike something you might enjoy with highly flavored Italian foods; a lighter red wine, such as a Nouveau Beaujolais in season, or a robust Chardonnay also make nice accompaniments to spicy dishes. And, there's always the oft unthought of Sangria, which can add a nice, fun touch to many adventurous meals. So, you see, a well-chosen wine can be enjoyed with a hot meal; don't spend a bundle on it, but try at least to get one with a cork.

Drunken Peppers

For a smokin' hot vodka martini, or an extra zippy bloody mary, dunk a few chile peppers in your bottle of hooch a day or two in advance. Start out with peppers that are in line with how spicy you want your concoction to turn out (remember, you may be serving this to guests, whatever that may mean to you), and take a nip every now and then to monitor the progress.

When you've got it just right, pull the peppers out (pour the whole mix through a strainer into a jar, then funnel it back into the bottle) and have a good old-fashioned taste test, followed by a good old-fashioned nap! Please remember to label the bottle to avoid giving your in-laws a surprise vodka tonic.

Sources

You can buy these and other hot sauces at a variety of sources: your local supermarket and farmer's market and various ethnic restaurants are your best bets. However, some sauces, such as the Pork Pit sauce, never travel commercially beyond their country of origin, which means you'll have to travel to obtain them. This is good news: go to these places if you can, get out of the tourist hotels and experience the native culture, and bring back all the hot sauce you can. It might be hot, dusty, or otherwise unpleasant where you are when you see a sauce, and you might not feel like going to the trouble of investigating it, haggling over the price, buying it, and then lugging it around the country, not to mention home. Make the effort! You will—and should—kick yourself when you get back to your air-conditioned home, with hot showers and cold beer, and think, why didn't I buy that when I had the chance? Skip the regrets—buy it!

There are also plenty of hot sauce mail-order houses cropping up in the United States. I've listed a few of them here. Also, check your phone book for specialty shops that sell little other than hot sauces—these stores are more common than you think. And, of course, mess around and make your own; it's your one opportunity to get exactly what you like, or at least to suppose that it will turn out that way.

One last piece of advice: subscribe to *Chile Pepper Magazine*, the best single, up-to-date source for information concerning hot sauces, spicy cuisine, and general information on what's happening, what's not, and what should be. The magazine's phone number is 1-800-959-5468.

Mo Hotta—Mo Betta
P.O. Box 4136
San Luis Obispo, CA 93403
1-800-462-3220
1-805-545-8389 (FAX)

Pendery's
1221 Manufacturing
Dallas, TX 75207-6506
1-800-533-1870

Salsa Express
100 North Tower Road
Alamo, TX 78516
1-800-SALSA

All Cajun Food Company
1019 Delcambre Road
Breaux Bridge, LA 70517
1-800-467-3613
1-318-332-1467 (FAX)

Old Southwest Trading Company
P.O. Box 7545
Albuquerque, NM 87194
1-505-836-0168
1-505-836-1682 (FAX)

Hot Sauce Harry's
3422 Flair Drive
Dallas, TX 75229
1-214-902-8552
1-214-956-9885 (FAX)

The Jalapeno Ranch
Fox Hollow Farm
3280 Flynn's Creek Road
Gainesboro, TN 38562
1-615-268-0672

Midwest Pepper Trading Company
3 Swannanoa Drive
Rochester, IL 62563
1-217-498-9233

Enchantment Spice and Specialty Food
P.O. Box 2598
Frisco, CO 80443
1-800-CHILI CO

Hot Shots
3124 Pinehurst Place
Charlotte, NC 28209
(local) 704-527-2422
1-800-248-5159

Tasting Notes

Use this space to jot down the names and pertinent information about sauces you've tasted and wish to buy, sauces you've bought and wish to remember, or sauces you've tasted and remember and wish never to buy again. The potential here is endless...

Sauce:

Comments:

Sauce:

Comments:

Sauce:

Comments:

Sauce:

Comments:

Sauce:

Comments:

Sauce:

Comments:

Sauce:

Comments:

Sauce:

Comments:

Tasting Notes

Sauce:

Comments:

Sauce:

Comments:

Sauce:

Comments:

Sauce:

Comments:

Sauce:

Comments:

Sauce:

Comments:

Thanks

I'd like to take a moment to thank a few people who played major roles in this book. First, my parents, for introducing me to hot sauce at a very young age—the local authorities would probably throw you in jail for child abuse these days, Dad! My wife Katherine, for her undying support of this admittedly strange project, for her willingness to forever alter her palate in the name of science, and for putting up with a very full refrigerator. Also, my mother-in-law, without whom my knowledge of peppers would be nil. Along the same vein, thanks to the cyber-surfers, whose pursuit of the ever-illusive piri piri was relentless, and much appreciated. Finally, to all of you who sat at my table on many occasions quietly bearing the cross of food too spicy to eat—well, thanks, and why didn't you just say something?!

Index of Hot Sauces

Index of Hot Sauces